EVENT MANAGEMENT *for* SPORTDIRECTORS

American Sport Education Program

Human Kinetics

of Congress Cataloging-in-Publication Data

American Sport Education Program.
     Event management for sportdirectors / American Sport Education
  Program.
        p.   cm.
     ISBN 0-87322-968-1 (spiral trade)
     1. Sports administration.   I. Title.
  GV713.A54   1996
  796'.06'9--dc20   95-21941
                                                                               CIP

ISBN: 0-87322-968-1

Copyright © 1996 by Human Kinetics Publishers, Inc.

Acquisitions Editor: Jim Kestner; **Contributing Author:** Jessica Daw; **Developmental Editor:** Jan Colarusso Seeley; **Assistant Editors:** Erin Cler and Ann Greenseth; **Editorial Assistants:** Amy Carnes, Jennifer Hemphill, and Andrew Starr; **Copyeditor:** Barbara K. Bergstrom; **Proofreader:** Sue Fetters; **Typesetter and Layout Artist:** Francine Hamerski; **Text and Cover Designer:** Stuart Cartwright; **Illustrator:** Stuart Cartwright; **Printer:** United Graphics

Printed in the United States of America   10 9 8 7 6 5 4 3 2 1

Human Kinetics
P.O. Box 5076, Champaign, IL 61825-5076
1-800-747-4457

Canada: Human Kinetics, Box 24040,
Windsor, ON N8Y 4Y9
1-800-465-7301 (in Canada only)

Europe: Human Kinetics
P.O. Box IW14, Leeds LS16 6TR, United Kingdom
(44) 1132 781708

Australia: Human Kinetics, 2 Ingrid Street,
Clapham 5062, South Australia
(08) 371 3755

New Zealand: Human Kinetics,
P.O. Box 105-231, Auckland 1
(09) 523 3462

Contents

*L*ist of Forms

Series Preface

The SportDirector Series is a revolutionary approach to the craft of managing athletic programs. Underlying the resources in this series is a set of principles drawn from a careful examination of the day-to-day responsibilities sport directors face. These principles have been framed as a sequence of tests, which each series resource has been designed to pass:

- Is the resource practical?
- Is it affordable?
- Does it save time?
- Is it easy to use?
- Is it up-to-date?
- Is it flexible enough to meet different programs' needs?
- Does using one resource from the series make it easier to use others?

To ensure that every resource passes these tests, we have worked closely with an editorial advisory board of prominent, experienced athletic directors from across the nation. With the board's assistance, we have developed the series to enable you to benefit from the latest thinking in directing sport programs. Each resource leads you carefully through three steps: planning, implementing, and evaluating.

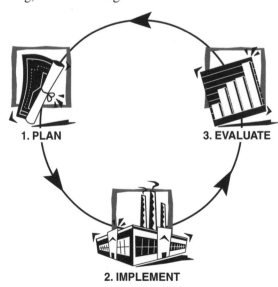

1. PLAN

3. EVALUATE

2. IMPLEMENT

What's so new about the approach? Nothing—until you actually apply it. That's where the series really breaks the mold. Besides telling you how important it is to plan for success in directing your programs, each resource will lead you step-by-step through that planning process. Forms and exercises will help you explore your role and philosophy within the organization, examine your particular needs, and then develop an effective plan of action. In each SportDirector resource these steps are applied specifically to the task at hand. For example, it is essential to assess your needs carefully as you carry out each of your program responsibilities: How you assess promotional needs, however, will differ significantly from how you assess personnel management needs. The series follows the same practical approach to lead you through the implementation and evaluation of your plan.

This approach is possible only because the series authors are experts not only in sport management but also in the specific areas they write about. With the help of the editorial advisory board, these authors translate their knowledge into practical, easy-to-follow recommendations, ready-to-use forms and checklists, and countless practical tips and examples so that you will come away with better ideas for directing your program. The authors also help you take advantage of the latest technology.

New and experienced interscholastic athletic directors alike will find that these resources take into account their widespread responsibilities and limited staff and funding assistance. Directors of Olympic National Governing Body club sport programs and other national and state sport directors will find valuable tools to enhance their efficiency and increase their effectiveness. Students of sport administration will find these resources valuable companions for understanding how to step into the field with confidence to succeed. And all sport directors will find that these tools help them to help the athletes, coaches, parents, and others in their organizational community.

Even more than a leader, you are the architect of your organization's athletic community. As you design and oversee the construction and maintenance of that community, you are in a unique position to ensure that the program achieves a common purpose. The SportDirector Series is conceived not only to help you attend to your everyday duties but also to coalesce your efforts to carry out your program's mission—to make your athletic community the best it can be.

—*Jim Kestner*

Credits

Form #2 Financial Planning Form
From *Youth SportDirector Guide* (pp. 5.16–5.18), by R. Martens, 1995, Champaign, IL: Human Kinetics. Copyright 1995 by Rainer Martens. Adapted with permission.

Form #3 Staff Planning Form
From *Youth SportDirector Guide* (pp. 6.57–6.60), by R. Martens, 1995, Champaign, IL: Human Kinetics. Copyright 1995 by Rainer Martens. Adapted with permission.

Form #4 Sample Coaching Application Form
From *Youth SportDirector Guide* (pp. 2.44–2.45), by R. Martens, 1995, Champaign, IL: Human Kinetics. Copyright 1995 by Rainer Martens. Reprinted with permission.

Form #5 Sample Coaching Interview Form
From *Youth SportDirector Guide* (pp. 2.46–2.47), by R. Martens, 1995, Champaign, IL: Human Kinetics. Copyright 1995 by Rainer Martens. Reprinted with permission.

Form #6 ASEP Coaching Appraisal Form
From *Youth SportDirector Guide* (pp. 2.50–2.51), by R. Martens, 1995, Champaign, IL: Human Kinetics. Copyright 1995 by Rainer Martens. Reprinted with permission.

Form #7 Designing Your Risk Management Plan
From *Youth SportDirector Guide* (pp. 4.44, 4.45–4.48), by R. Martens, 1995, Champaign, IL: Human Kinetics. Copyright 1995 by Rainer Martens. Adapted with permission.

Form #8 Sample Waiver/Release Form
From *Sport, Physical Activity, and the Law* (pp. 239–240), by N.J. Dougherty, D. Auxter, A.S. Goldberger, and G.S. Heinzmann, 1994, Champaign, IL: Human Kinetics. Copyright 1994 by Neil J. Dougherty, David Auxter, Alan S. Goldberger, and Gregg S. Heinzmann. Adapted with permission.

Form #9 Sample Emergency Care and Transportation Consent Form
From *Youth SportDirector Guide* (p. 4.35), by R. Martens, 1995, Champaign, IL: Human Kinetics. Copyright 1995 by Rainer Martens. Adapted with permission.

Form #10 Sample Registration Entry Form
Reprinted with the permission of the Champaign Park District, Champaign, IL.

Form #11 Sample Facility Rental Agreement
From *Youth SportDirector Guide* (pp. 6.51–6.52), by R. Martens, 1995, Champaign, IL: Human Kinetics. Copyright 1995 by Rainer Martens. Adapted with permission.

Form #12 Sample Facility Inspection Checklist
From *Youth SportDirector Guide* (pp. 4.25–4.28), by R. Martens, 1995, Champaign, IL: Human Kinetics. Copyright 1995 by Rainer Martens. Adapted with permission.
From *American Coaching Effectiveness Program Level 2 Sport Law Workbook* (pp. 40–41), by American Coaching Effectiveness Program, 1985, Champaign, IL: Human Kinetics. Copyright 1985 by Human Kinetics Publishers, Inc. Adapted with permission.
From "Safety Checklists: Making Indoor Areas Hazard-Free," by J.R. Olson, 1985, *Athletic Business*, **9**(11), pp. 36–38. Copyright 1985 by Athletic Business Magazine. Adapted with permission.

Form #13a Sample Inventory Form A
From *Youth SportDirector Guide* (p. 6.53), by R. Martens, 1995, Champaign, IL: Human Kinetics. Copyright 1995 by Rainer Martens. Reprinted with permission.

Form #13b Sample Inventory Form B
From *Youth SportDirector Guide* (p. 6.54), by R. Martens, 1995, Champaign, IL: Human Kinetics. Copyright 1995 by Rainer Martens. Reprinted with permission.

Form #15 Equipment Inspection Checklist
From *Youth SportDirector Guide* (pp. 4.29–4.32), by R. Martens, 1995, Champaign, IL: Human Kinetics. Copyright 1995 by Rainer Martens. Adapted with permission.

Introduction

As a sport director, you have many responsibilities. Unfortunately, the planning and managing of events sometimes leaves you feeling overwhelmed by this aspect of your job alone. You develop schedules for one or more sports, conduct a team fundraiser, plan to host a preseason tournament and state championship, then tackle an intramural or club league—and that's just for starters. For every event, you plan finances, recruit volunteers, hire officials, develop risk and emergency plans, and sort through enough papers to make finding your desktop a 2-day job. Sometimes the numerous considerations for even one event can be mind-boggling!

Event Management for SportDirectors is designed as a hands-on tool for planning events in a systematic and organized manner. Just as importantly, it provides you with the peace of mind that comes from knowing you have a plan to track the seemingly endless details that can make event management difficult. This tool will help you discover ways to avoid doing everything yourself—and still get it done right. Best of all, you will find *Event Management for SportDirectors* easy to use. Once you use it, you'll wonder how you ever got along without it!

Planning an event is deciding in advance what to do, how to do it, when to do it, and who to get to do it. Plans are your road map for reaching your goals. If your plans are vague, you'll take an indirect route or get lost trying to get there. If they are wrong, you will not reach your goal. Good plans will get you to your destination, although sometimes you'll run into obstacles along the way. Then you'll need to detour—adjust your plans based on the circumstances—to reach your goal. Approach revising your plans with the same enthusiasm you brought to developing your original plans. Successful events occur because of appropriate prior planning.

HOW TO USE *EVENT MANAGEMENT FOR SPORTDIRECTORS*

When there is much to plan and organize, a checklist of tasks to complete is essential. The American Sport Education Program's (ASEP) *Event Management for SportDirectors* is a comprehensive checklist of categories and tasks to be completed in planning and conducting a sport event. In preparing the Event Management guide, we considered individual and team sports; regular events such as interscholastic league play, club play, and intramurals; special events such as tournaments and all-star games; and small and large events. The tasks are organized into logical categories, and each task is explained briefly with suggestions to consider during the planning process. When it is helpful, we also include additional sources of information about the task and sample forms that you can modify to suit your needs.

Event Management for SportDirectors is made up of 18 major categories such as Financial Planning, Risk and Emergency Plans, and Facilities Planning. Each category presents a series of tasks to complete. Depending on the type of event you are hosting, any particular category may or may not apply. And within a specific category, any of the listed tasks may or may not apply to your event. Here's how to use the Event Management guide:

1. Before tackling any event planning, make a copy of the categories on pages 1 to 52 and the forms on pages 55 to 91 to keep as a template. This template will serve as your master copy as you plan other events in the future.

2. Read through the entire guide. If you have not managed an event before, don't be overwhelmed by what appears at first to be an endless amount of work. If you are planning a small event, many of the tasks will not be applicable. If you're planning a large event, there's more reason to do the planning thoroughly so that you can delegate the work to others. Also, don't forget to utilize the experiences of veteran sport directors. Most seasoned sport directors will be happy to share successful event management strategies.

3. As you review the categories of tasks, you'll likely find some that are not appropriate for your event; perhaps even entire categories will not be relevant. You may also have planning tasks that we did not include or that are unique to your event that you should add to the guide. Form 1, Event Planning Checklist, on page 55 presents a list of categories involved in managing an event. As you read through the guide, consider each category and determine whether or not it applies to your event. Once you've determined this, put a check in the appropriate column. If you aren't sure, check the question mark column and come back to that category once you've gathered more information about your event. If you need more detail regarding a particular category or the tasks within, refer to the page reference where the category can be found. Use the extra spaces at the end of the form to add categories that we have not included in the guide (you may not realize what these categories are yet, so don't worry if you have to add them later).

4. Next, go through the copy of the Event Management guide that you made for yourself and mark out the categories that don't apply to your event. Within the categories that do apply, mark out any tasks that are not appropriate. Your goal is to create a worksheet that contains only the categories of tasks needed for this event.

5. Now begin with the first category, Planning the Event Objectives, on page 1. Read the introduction to the category, and then read the first task and its explanation. Respond to that task as completely as you can, recording your response in the space provided. Your response may take many forms, including a plan of action, a delegation of task, or simply a reply statement. If you need more information in responding to this task, make a note about what it is you need to find out. Continue this for the rest of the tasks in this category. When you finish this category, continue with the subsequent categories.

6. When appropriate, use the space following each task to indicate the start date and complete date for each task. In some cases, this step may not be necessary since your task response may be a reply statement (e.g., replying to the Determine the type of event task with a statement that this event is for the top four basketball teams in the conference as determined by regular season standings). When time lines are necessary, the complete date is the date by which the task needs to be finished. The start date represents the date you feel work on the task should begin. Identifying start and complete dates, when

appropriate, will help you plan both a realistic time line for completing your plans and monitoring your progress in planning the event.

7. Recognize that the way you plan each task may influence other tasks. For example, you may plan a large event with terrific awards, but when you complete your budget you'll find you can't afford them. Thus, you'll need to revise your plans for the scope of the event and the awards to be given.

8. As you work through the Event Management guide, use the Financial Planning Form, Form 2, on page 56 and the Staff Planning Form, Form 3, on page 59 to detail your specific needs in these two areas.

9. Share your completed event management plan with those who will benefit from reading it or be able to help you in further planning or conducting the event.

To illustrate how the Event Management guide works in practice, we created a hypothetical event and used the guide to plan it (see Appendix A). Feel free to refer to this example as you read through the categories and tasks.

This Event Management guide will help you develop a specific plan to manage any event. With this prior planning, your event will be organized and successful from the very beginning!

1. PLANNING THE EVENT OBJECTIVES

Complete the tasks below if you are responsible for determining the objectives of an event. The size of the event might lead you to form a committee to help you. A committee approach can assure you that the objectives identified are the most appropriate. Also, when establishing objectives, be sure to consider other factors that could impact your objectives, such as finances and facilities, for example. If the objectives of the event are already determined, record your interpretations of the objectives here and share them with those who decided the original objectives to be sure that you are in agreement. Share the objectives with those who help you conduct the event.

A. Determine the type of event.

The event could be league competition involving various club teams, interscholastic or intramural league play over a season, a one-day or weekend tournament, a match, a meet, an all-star game, or something else. Describe specifically the type of event you will hold. If it is an event where teams will be involved, be specific on how they will be formed (e.g., based on friends, skill level, tryouts, etc.).

Your response: _____

_____

_____

_____

Start date: _____   Complete date: _____

B. Determine for whom the event is planned.

Be sure that all those responsible for planning the event agree on who should participate. Is it an intramural event for students of your school only, or is it an interscholastic event in which other schools will participate? Is it for members of your club only, or will you compete against other club teams? Age range, gender, academic requirements, special needs, and qualifications of the participants need to be considered. Are there other criteria that include or exclude participants for this event?

Your response: _____

_____

_____

_____

Start date: _____   Complete date: _____

C. Determine the size or scope of the event.

While the size and scope of your event will many times be predetermined, in some cases they will not be determined, particularly in the case of intramurals and club events. To help determine the facility and equipment needs, personnel requirements, and budget, you will need to set some limits on how many participants or teams your event will involve. Set criteria on how the limit will be reached (e.g., first come, first served; number of teams or participants; past participation in the event; tryouts; etc.).

Your response: _____

_____

_____

_____

Start date: _____   Complete date: _____

D. Determine the categories of competition to be offered.

Decide how you will organize the competition so it is safe and challenging for all involved. This will depend on the type of event you're planning (i.e., interscholastic tournament, club tournament, intramurals). Will different categories of competition, such as varsity, junior varsity, A, B, competitive, or recreational, be offered? When organizing competitive events, consider such factors as age, gender, grade, height, weight, skill level, qualifications through previous play, and disability.

Your response: _____

_____

_____

_____

Start date: _____   Complete date: _____

E. Determine the dates and duration of the event.

Consider these factors when deciding on the duration of the event and specific dates:

- Number of days needed to complete the competition and still allow participants adequate rest between contests (including travel time)
- Number, availability, cost, and size of facilities
- Convenience of the dates for participants, coaches, officials, and other personnel
- Transportation needs
- Availability of officials and other personnel to conduct the event
- Weather or weather provisions
- Competing events and holidays

- Probability of delays, cancellations, rain-outs, and conflicting events
- A refund policy in the event of cancellation or postponement

When determining dates and duration of event, remember that there is no perfect date—any date will be problematic for some people. Try to select the date that will best serve the majority.

Your response: _____

_____

_____

_____

Start date: _____   Complete date: _____

F. Determine the location(s) of the event.

The event may require a single location with a facility that you control, making this task easy to complete. On the other hand, the event may require multiple sites for completing all contests, contracts with other agencies for obtaining rights to facilities, and a transportation system for moving participants from one site to another—all these details make the planning far more complex. Evaluate whether your community, school, or club facility is the best location for this event or if another community, school, or club with better facilities, weather, or housing availability would be more suitable.

Your response: _____

_____

_____

_____

Start date: _____   Complete date: _____

2. FINANCIAL PLANNING

Although money should not be the most important planning concern, finances play a major part in feasibility—they help determine the "parameters of the event." Thus, a preliminary financial plan is necessary at this stage because your budget will influence your subsequent planning. It's also important to think about equity and fairness when distributing finances. Then, as you plan the steps in the other categories, you can be more precise in your financial estimates, permitting you to refine your budget. If the event is large, consider either assigning or hiring a financial manager to assist you or developing a finance committee to oversee the financial aspects of this event. Extra unplanned expenses will always crop up. Consider establishing or utilizing an Emergency Fund or Administrative Account to meet these unexpected expenses during the event. Be able to justify your budgets to the public, since they are considered open information and can be reviewed under the Freedom of Information Act.

A. Prepare a budget for the event.

Use the budget model template in Form 2 on page 56 to develop the categories for income and expenses for the event. First, determine which categories of funds are or may be sources of income for your event. Separate these income estimates into two categories: committed funds and potential funds. *Committed* funds are those that you know are available to you for this event—for example, budgeted funds by your school district, registration fees, and sponsorships. *Potential* funds are good monetary prospects not yet locked up. Obtaining the funds will require additional steps—e.g., sponsorships, admission fees, donations, fundraising events, or food sales. If you have conducted this event before, start budget planning by looking at your past financial records from that event. Don't assume, though, that the previous event's committed expenses are still forthcoming; confirm this first with the source.

Next, enter the expenses for conducting the events and calculate the difference between the anticipated income and expenses. Compare the committed funds to expenses first. If these funds cover the expenses, then you have no financial worries. If the committed funds do not cover your expenses, then determine if the committed and potential funds combined cover your expenses. If they do not, you obviously need to plan for reducing your expenses or increasing income. If the combination does cover your expenses, calculate the amount that comes from potential funds and give careful thought to the probability of obtaining these funds. Continue revising your budget as you obtain more accurate information about the funds available and actual expenses.

Your response: _____

_____

_____

_____

Start date: _____   Complete date: _____

B. Develop plans to obtain all income and implement these plans.

First, take any necessary steps to obtain the committed funds. (If these funds are from registration fees, then be certain you have plans for collecting these fees in the registration category of this guide.) Second, develop specific plans for obtaining the potential funds from each source of income identified in Form 2 and then implement those plans. If the event is unexpected, such as qualifying for post-season competition, you may need to have a special fundraising event. It is especially important to organize and to supervise this fundraising task effectively. See the information below for assistance with special event fundraising.

Your response: _____

_____

_____

_____

Start date: _____ Complete date: _____

C. Keep accurate records.

You will want to set up a record keeping system for income and expenses. Keep the income and expenses completely separate from your personal finances so that there is no impropriety or appearance thereof. You may even want to consider having a separate committee to handle all funds to help guard against financial impropriety or conflicts of interest. If others collect income, you need a system of receipts and verifications of income received with income deposited. If others are permitted to make expenditures, you need a system for authorizing the type and amount of expenditures, verifying the expenditure, and recording it, as well as a system for team travel-cash advances. Consider procedures for assessing financial records after the event. See the following information on simple record keeping systems.

Your response: _____

_____

_____

_____

Start date: _____ Complete date: _____

Special Event Fundraising

Special event fundraising is distinguished from other methods of accruing funds in that you provide people with a product or service for which they are willing to pay. When considering a fundraising event, check the timing of other fundraisers in the community to prevent conflicts. Make sure to obtain approval for the fundraiser from the principal.

Numerous special events that can be used to raise funds are fun and profitable. For example, you can conduct

- food sales (bake sales, fruit, candy),
- service sales (car washes, clean-up work, recyclables collections),
- auctions,
- raffles and lotteries,
- social events (parties, dances, and balls),
- camps and clinics,
- activity-a-thons (walking, swimming, running, biking, dancing),
- eating events (banquets, pie eating contests, celebrity dinners, pancake feeds),
- celebrity sport contests (softball, basketball, golf, tennis),
- entertainment (shows, exhibits, benefit productions), and
- publishing (production of cookbooks, newsletters, and directories).

If you think fundraising is a way to help you pay for your program or event, then we recommend you purchase the following book:

Stier, W.F. (1993). *Fund Raising in Sport and Recreation.* Human Kinetics, P.O. Box 5076, Champaign, IL 61825 (800-747-4457). This book includes 70 fundraising activities organized into four parts by the amount of funds the event can potentially generate ($0 to $3,000, $3000-$5,000, $5,000-$10,000, and $10,000+). Stier explains how you can conduct the event, what resources you need, how you decide the complexity of the event, and what risks you might incur.

Managing a fundraising event is similar to conducting a sport event. As the administrator or director, you need to perform many of the same tasks as for a sport event, but for a different purpose. If you decide to conduct a fundraising event, adapt this Event Management guide to help you plan the event. Fundraising can be a good source of income for your program when you do the following:

1. Have a good image in the community.
2. Plan an event that appeals to sufficiently large numbers of people.
3. Organize the event effectively.
4. Promote the fundraiser well.
5. Select a time for your fundraiser that does not compete with other events and that allows many people to attend.
6. Avoid events that involve considerable up-front expenses that risk a potential loss.
7. Have the financial resources to fund the up-front costs.
8. Have the support and help of the members of your organization to conduct the event.

Record Keeping

The record keeping system you need depends on how large a program you have and what your supervisor and/or district may require of you. Three simple record keeping ideas follow.

1. You can create your own complete "paper" system that builds in some checks and balances and lets you categorize income and expenses more completely. This is beneficial if you want to compare actual income and expenses with what you budgeted, which is not a bad idea to do. We recommend two books to help you set up your own system:

- Ragan, R.C. (1992). *Step-By-Step Bookkeeping*. New York: Sterling Publishing.
- Pinson, L., & Jinnett, J. (1993). *Keeping the Books*. Dover, NH: Upstart.

2. If you prefer not to set up your own set of books, you can purchase printed bookkeeping systems for small business that work very nicely. Dome Industries produces weekly and monthly ledgers that will help you keep track of income and expenses, deductions, payroll for up to 25 employees, important tax dates, net profit, and more. Providence Business Forms also produces a general ledger and trial balance book. A local office supply store should carry these products, that cost under $15, or you can contact these companies directly. Dome Industries, 10 New England Way, Warwick, RI 02886 (1-800-432-4352). Providence Business Forms, 96 Rolfe Square, Cranston, RI 02910 (401-941-2500).

3. You can keep your records on the computer. We recommend a software program by Intuit called *Quicken*. It's the easiest user-friendly program we've seen. Over a million people use it for their personal financial records, and it has a business option that works ideally for an interscholastic or club sports program. When you set up the *Quicken* accounts, use those that you selected for your budget, and you're in business. This versatile software package gives you all the tools you need to manage your event's finances, as well as your overall program finances. Here are just some of the tasks that *Quicken* can help you complete:

- Set up and adjust a budget for your income and expenses.
- Keep track of tax-related activities—earnings, deductions, and so on.
- Track all your financial activity and automatically update the register and balances.
- Print payroll checks and pay bills electronically.
- Generate customized reports for income and expenses, cash flow, balance sheets, and budget.

Use *Quicken* to organize your program's finances, and you'll see how quick and easy it is to keep track of where the money goes. *Quicken* is available wherever software is sold and costs about $60.

3. RULES AND OFFICIALS PLANS

You will need to make decisions about the rules you will use to govern the event. These rules should cover participant eligibility, the playing of the contests, and managing disputes and unsportsmanlike behavior. You will also need to determine how to officiate the contests and what officials you will need (e.g., referees, scorekeepers, timers, judges, etc.). Commonly the person coordinating the officials is responsible for directing the rules planning. Having a tournament or event director make final decisions on rules disputes is a good idea.

A. Select the eligibility rules to follow.

Depending on the type of event, the eligibility rules can be those of your school, an athletic conference, the state activities association, or national governing body (or any combination thereof). These rules should be clearly written out and distributed to all involved.

Your response: _____

_____

_____

_____

Start date: _____   Complete date: _____

B. Decide what contest rules to use.

Most club teams play by an established set of rules (or modification thereof) determined by the national governing body of their sport. An athletic conference or a state activities or athletic association as well as the National Federation of State High School Associations determine rules for most interscholastic sports competitions. For intramural activities, you may determine appropriate rules to use in conducting your event or league. A useful reference is Jess R. White's *Sports Rules Encyclopedia*, available from Human Kinetics, P.O. Box 5076, Champaign, IL 61825 (800-747-4457). This revised and greatly expanded second edition includes the rules to 52 sports. You'll find the official rules of play as approved by the governing body, specifications for the playing area, requirements for equipment, and more.

Your response: _____

_____

_____

_____

Start date: _____   Complete date: _____

C. Modify rules to suit your event.

If the event is part of sanctioned competition conducted through a conference or state association, you may not be allowed to modify the rules. However, when you can, modify rules to improve safety or to assure equitable competition in accordance with the limitations of a facility, the equipment, the time, and participant abilities. Be sure to communicate all rule modifications to those involved in the event.

Your response: _____

_____

_____

_____

Start date: _____ Complete date: _____

D. Determine who will officiate the contests and secure their services.

Depending on the event, decide if volunteers are sufficiently qualified or can be trained to officiate the contests or if it would be best to contract with trained, experienced officials. Check with the athletic conference, state association, or national governing body to determine minimum requirements officials must meet for the particular event you're holding. Be sure you obtain the services of officials well in advance and that you have a liability waiver and contract or letter of agreement that states what dates they will be officiating, how many contests they will officiate, how much payment they will receive, and what happens if the event is cancelled or postponed. If the event is large, consider developing an officials committee to obtain, schedule, and supervise officials. When working with officials groups, be sure to consider their hidden costs such as booking fees.

Your response: _____

_____

_____

Start date: _____ Complete date: _____

E. Determine what other officials you need (e.g., scorekeepers, timers, judges, and announcers) and plan to obtain their services.

Depending on the sport, you may need little or considerable help to conduct the event properly. Plan your needs now and then see the Staff Planning Form (Form 3, page 59) and the Staffing Plans section on pages 49–52 for further tasks to complete. If your event has the potential to expand, have a contingency plan in place to secure more staff if necessary.

Your response: _____

_____

_____

Start date: _____ Complete date: _____

F. Determine whether a pre-event coach and officials meeting is needed.

In interscholastic tournament competitions, and possibly club tournaments, it's a good idea to have a pre-event meeting to review all rules with staff, coaches, and officials. Consider making available to all coaches a rules packet that specifies all tournament rules in writing.

Your response: _____

_____

_____

Start date: _____   Complete date: _____

G. Determine the procedures to follow when a protest is made by a player, coach, or team official.

Many sports have complex rules enforced by officials who must make judgments about events during the contest. Participants will inevitably disagree with some of these judgments and rule interpretations. Many sports rules specify procedures for protesting various rules, but you may want to modify these procedures. For events that include interscholastic competition, you may want to put together a committee of impartial people to settle all protests and rule disputes.

Your response: _____

_____

_____

Start date: _____   Complete date: _____

H. Determine the procedures to follow when participants, coaches, and/or spectators display unsportsmanlike behavior or engage in criminal acts.

Many national governing bodies, athletic conferences, and state associations, as well as the National Federation of State High School Associations, have statements regarding unsportsmanlike behavior by coaches and players. If the rules do not cover this area, you'll need to develop a set of procedures and communicate them to all involved. You should also have clear guidelines specifying when an individual's behavior crosses the line between being unsportsmanlike to being criminal or potentially criminal. Establish when to call in the appropriate law enforcement agency for such actions as damage to property, illegal use of alcohol and other drugs, stealing, threats of violence, and actual violence.

Your response: _____

_____

_____

Start date: _____   Complete date: _____

4. COACH DEVELOPMENT PLANS

In most cases, the events you're planning won't require obtaining and/or educating coaches. But if the event you're planning (i.e., intramurals or club sports) will require these and similar tasks, this section will be useful in helping you plan for these.

A. Develop plans for recruiting coaches.

Determine how you are going to obtain your coaches and identify important criteria the candidates must meet. Consider including plans to obtain a pool of coaches, as well as to select coaches once you've got a pool of candidates. A Sample Coaching Application Form (Form 4) and a Sample Coaching Interview Form (Form 5) are included on pages 62–65.

Your response: _____

_____

_____

_____

Start date: _____   Complete date: _____

B. Develop plans for educating your coaches.

Once you have selected your coaches, the single most important activity you can do to insure positive experiences for your athletes is to provide quality educational programs for your coaches. Your coaching education program should include

- your program philosophy;
- fundamental principles of coaching, including sport psychology, biomechanics, pedagogy, sport physiology, and legal aspects of sport;
- techniques and tactics of the sport;
- injury prevention and first aid for first responders (the ASEP Leader Level/NFICEP courses can be used to meet the preceding coaching education components);
- organizational procedures regarding equipment and facility usage, financial procedures, travel procedures, and utilization of support staff; and
- for returning and experienced coaches, more advanced coach education resources in the areas of administration, pedagogy, sport psychology, nutrition and weight control, sport physiology, and biomechanics (consider ASEP's Master Level resources for meeting these needs).

For a complete list of ASEP educational resources, see Appendix B.

Your response: _____

_____

_____

_____

Start date: _____   Complete date: _____

C. Develop plans for evaluating your coaches.

Now that you've selected your coaches and provided them with educational opportunities, giving positive constructive feedback is an excellent way to maintain their motivation to learn and to continue coaching. In what areas is it important to evaluate coaches, and how will you conduct evaluations? An ASEP Coaching Appraisal Form (Form 6) is included on page 66. Also, consider using the following "Ten Commandments for Providing Coaching Feedback" as a guide to positive communication with coaches.

Your response: _____

_____

_____

_____

Start date: _____   Complete date: _____

Ten Commandments for Providing Coaching Feedback

1. Establish that your feedback is designed to be *constructive*, that your purpose is to help coaches provide a better sport experience for the participants.

2. Be sincere in your remarks, conveying verbally and nonverbally that you wish to help. Show respect and understanding throughout the discussion.

3. Begin by complimenting the coaches on those aspects of their coaching behaviors that were done well. Identify specific coaching behaviors that you observed.

4. Provide positive reinforcement for coaches' behaviors, not the outcomes of their behaviors. For example, praise the effective teaching of skills rather than the actual winning of games.

5. Be direct in your comments; don't be wishy-washy when providing constructive criticism. Know what you want to say. Then point out what you saw that could be improved and make recommendations on how to make the improvement.

6. Always recognize coaches for their volunteered time and their positive intentions. Try to praise such intangibles as the demonstration of good judgment, self-control, and responsibility.

7. Give coaches an opportunity to share their thoughts about the evaluation and how to improve their coaching behaviors.

8. Use good judgment in selecting an appropriate time and place for providing constructive criticism. Do not provide constructive criticism when coaches are busy, emotional, or engaged with other people.

9. Avoid providing feedback if you are angry, irritated, or emotional about the coaches' behaviors. Delay the feedback until you have time to regain control and put things in perspective.

10. End the feedback session on a positive note. Refocus attention on what the coaches did well and the value of their services to the community.

5. RISK AND EMERGENCY PLANS

It is a good idea to analyze risks and develop a plan for reducing the chance of injury to those participating in or attending the event. The steps you take to reduce the risk of harm will also reduce the likelihood of a lawsuit. As part of a risk plan, you need to plan for emergencies.

A. Prepare a risk management plan for this event.

Preparing a risk management plan will help you to provide the safest and fairest environment possible for your event participants. Your risk management plan should include inspection of facilities, equipment, housing areas, and all transportation aspects of the event; the presence of properly trained and educated coaches, officials, volunteers, and participants; as well as proper supervision over all aspects of events. Form 7 on page 68 will help you develop a risk management plan.

Your response: _____

_____

_____

_____

Start date: _____   Complete date: _____

B. Determine if you should use a waiver or release form.

If you can reduce your risk of lawsuit by using a waiver/release form, make copies of the form for all participants to complete during registration. Adapt the sample in Form 8 on page 73 to suit your purposes.

Your response: _____

_____

_____

_____

Start date: _____   Complete date: _____

C. Determine if you need an emergency care and transportation consent form.

If you determine that this form is needed, make copies for all participants to complete during registration. Use or adapt Form 9 on page 75 for this purpose.

Your response: _____

_____

_____

_____

Start date: _____   Complete date: _____

D. Determine your need for insurance to reduce your risk in managing this event.

Contact the risk manager at your school district or organization to determine if your usual insurance coverage is adequate. If it is not, purchase additional insurance for this event. Inform all appropriate personnel what insurance coverage is provided.

Your response: _____

_____

_____

_____

Start date: _____   Complete date: _____

E. Determine if you will be in compliance with local fire and safety ordinances for this event.

Call the officials in your area to find out what regulations affect your event. If this is an ongoing event, keep a file regarding compliance with local fire and safety regulations. Prior to the event, contact the fire marshal and rescue squad. Send a map with access areas illustrated. On event days, be sure all fire lanes and entrance gates are not blocked by cars or other objects.

Your response: _____

_____

_____

_____

Start date: _____   Complete date: _____

F. If food is to be sold, determine what steps are necessary for compliance with local or state food inspection laws.

Contact your local health department to find out what regulations pertain to your event.

Your response: _____

_____

_____

_____

Start date: _____   Complete date: _____

G. Prepare an emergency plan for this event.

The emergency plan should specify how players and others will be treated if injured. It should include where the nearest phone is located, how emergency personnel will be contacted when needed, what medical personnel and supplies will be present at the event's first aid station, how injured persons will be transported to emergency care facilities, and who is responsible for supervising an emergency. Some considerations for developing your emergency plan follow.

Your response: _____

_____

_____

_____

Start date: _____   Complete date: _____

H. Develop a plan for managing spectators if large numbers are expected.

Because some interscholastic and club sports events attract large numbers of spectators, you will need to plan for them. Factors to consider include adequate seating for spectators, alternate plans in case of inclement weather, sufficient restrooms for both sexes, food services for snackers, consistent supervision of facilities, and concrete plans for safety and security (crowd control). Also consider policies for band and cheerleader involvement, as well as home-event decoration policies. Other sections of this Event Management guide will indicate planning tasks if sufficient spectators are expected.

Your response: _____

_____

_____

_____

Start date: _____   Complete date: _____

Considerations for Developing an Emergency Plan

Immediate care for an injured participant or spectator is of the utmost importance for ensuring the best care and maintaining a safe environment. These people listed should respond to the needs of an injured participant or spectator:

- Team or on-site physician
- Team or on-site trainer
- Emergency medical personnel
- Coach

Depending on the size and scope of the event, having appropriate medical personnel available to treat participants and spectators is critical. Pay particular attention to the number of medical personnel needed, their placement, communication systems, and transportation systems.

If an injury does occur, follow this sequence of emergency steps:

1. Assess the injury.
2. Send your contact person to activate the emergency medical response plan. If the injured party is a minor, call the parents.
3. Administer basic first aid.
4. Help emergency medical personnel prepare to transport the injured party to the medical facility.
5. Designate someone to go with the injured party. This escort person should be responsible, calm, and acquainted with them. Assistant coaches or parents are good candidates for this job.
6. Complete an injury report form while the details of the incident are still fresh in your mind.

6. REGISTRATION PLANS

Depending on the event, you will likely need to have a registration period to obtain eligible candidates or teams to participate. You need to plan this part of the event carefully so that you obtain all the information you need during registration and you make the registration process convenient for those participating and efficient for you.

A. Determine the "qualifiers" for participation in the event.

Is this event open to everyone, or are there "qualifiers"? Some events may be restricted to only those who have achieved a particular time, distance, or record for instance. Determine if qualifying criteria are needed and, if so, what the criteria are.

Your response: _____

_____

_____

_____

Start date: _____   Complete date: _____

B. Determine what information you need to get during registration.

Review the following list of information you may need for individual and team registration.

- Name, address, gender, birth date, age, height, and weight of participant(s)/team members
- Information about parents
- Evidence of eligibility and/or proof of residency
- Identification as a national governing body member
- Notification of special services required by individuals
- Sizes for fitting of equipment
- Collection of any fees
- Waiver/release form
- Medical history
- Emergency care and transportation consent form

Your response: _____

_____

_____

_____

Start date: _____   Complete date: _____

C. Determine when the registration period begins and ends.

Consider whether it is better to have a short or long registration period. This may depend on the estimated number of registrants and how many registrations you will have to process. It may also depend on how quickly you must have the information to schedule the competition. Set up a timetable for this process. Make sure your registration or entry deadline is clearly stated so all interested participants will know when they must submit their registration materials.

Your response: _____

_____

_____

_____

Start date: _____   Complete date: _____

D. Determine the registration process to be followed.

Plan a way for potential participants to receive registration or entry forms and to return the forms to you or your office. Will you accept mailed or telephoned registrations or entries, or will registration take place only at a certain location? How much help will you need to process the registrations or entries, and what will each helper's assignment be? How many registrations/entries will you accept? How will you process the registration information to assign players to teams, teams to leagues, leagues to playing facilities, and so on? Will receipts need to be issued to those events requiring entry fees?

Your response: _____

_____

_____

_____

Start date: _____   Complete date: _____

E. Prepare the appropriate forms for the registration process.

Form 10 on page 76 offers a sample form for obtaining the usual information from an individual registering to join a league. Adapt it to suit your purposes.

Your response: _____

_____

_____

_____

Start date: _____   Complete date: _____

7. SCHEDULING PLANS

This category of tasks involves not only the dates of the event but also the scheduling of practices and contests for participants. If facilities are at a premium, which they often are, you may need a system for scheduling practice times. If planning a season schedule, in each task that follows consider other activities that schedule the same playing and practice areas. You may want to develop a usage priority list based on which sports are in-season, but make sure you can justify this usage schedule as fair and equitable. For a "one-shot" event (competition completed over the course of a day or weekend), the scheduling of contests can involve such duties as making league round-robin schedules, double-elimination tournament brackets, pairings for a wrestling meet, and so on. Scheduling the contests may be simple or quite complex, depending on the event. A good reference on this subject is John Byl's *Organizing Successful Tournaments*, available from Human Kinetics, P.O. Box 5076, Champaign, IL 61825 (800-747-4457). This book will help you work through the mind-twisting combinations of tournament players and games. Chapters are devoted to five major tournament types—single elimination, multilevel, double elimination, round robin, and extended—and their variations.

A. Determine the facilities available and compute the maximum number of practices and contests that can be held.

Investigate the current facilities schedule for possible conflicting events. If you anticipate needing more facilities than are available to you, determine if you can get access to other facilities in the area. Once you've determined which facilities will be used, compute the maximum number of practices and contests that can be held.

Your response: _____

_____

_____

_____

Start date: _____   Complete date: _____

B. Determine the time of day to schedule practices and contests.

After identifying the maximum number of practices and contests that can be held at the facilities, determine actual practice and competition times. Plan "catch-up" time for events that may go into overtime, extra innings, and so on. Don't forget to plan for maintenance time, as well as inclement weather, with cancellation procedures and a refund policy, if necessary. In case of unexpected occurrences, consider other options, such as cutting the event short, rescheduling it for another date, delaying the event, and so on.

Your response: _____

_____

_____

_____

Start date: _____   Complete date: _____

C. Compute the actual number of practices and contests to be played during your event and develop a schedule.

Set up a schedule book or purchase one of the many software packages on the market that make it easier to schedule practices and contests in many different formats. Packages range from $300 to $1,800. Here are three to check out: *All American SportsWare*, 90 High Street, Newtown, PA 18940 (215-860-8535); *RecWare* by Sierra Digital, 937 Enterprise Drive, Sacramento, CA 95825 (916-925-9096); and A.E. Klawitter, 5005 Newport Drive, Suite 510, Rolling Meadows, IL 60008.

Your response: _____

_____

_____

_____

Start date: _____   Complete date: _____

D. Determine the need to schedule practice times because of facility demand.

If you determine that to be fair and reduce disputes you need to schedule practice times, then you'll need to develop such a schedule. In doing so, consider the availability of the facilities, the days of the week and times of the day to schedule practices, the actual number of practices that can be held, and any other factors that may influence the schedule. For example, you may want to choose early times and smaller sites for younger teams (e.g., junior varsity, ninth-grade, B, or A teams) and later times and larger sites for older teams (e.g., varsity, senior intramurals, AA, or AAA teams). If so, arrange your practice schedule accordingly.

Your response: _____

_____

_____

_____

Start date: _____   Complete date: _____

E. Prepare the schedule for the contests.

Consider these factors when preparing the schedule:

- The facilities available for contests.
- How long each contest will take.
- The maximum number of contests that can be held with these facilities.
- The actual number of contests to be played for this event.
- How much rest is required between contests.
- Determine a method to make the competition as equitable as possible. For example, you may seed players or teams in tournaments, use a handicap system such as in golf or bowling, create classes based on ability, or have qualifying rounds to determine who advances to further competition. Plan for postponements, forfeits, and delays in the schedule by building some catch-up time into the schedule.
- Will contracts with opposing teams be necessary? If so, prepare contracts and establish time lines for contract returns.
- Does this sport typically offer guarantees to visiting opponents? If so, determine what the guarantee will be and include the information in the contract.

Your response: _____

_____

_____

_____

Start date: _____   Complete date: _____

F. Print and distribute the schedule.

Once the schedule is complete, have it copied and distribute it to all who need to see it. Participants, coaches, parents, officials, and those assisting in conducting the event will need a copy. You may want to place a qualifying statement on your schedule indicating that the schedule is subject to change and that all participants will be notified of any changes. Don't forget to provide schedules for the facility staff, maintenance staff, custodial staff, and so on. If many spectators are expected, you may want to develop a program that contains the schedule and some information about the contestants. If the event is a tournament, plan how to update the schedule and make the information available to participants and spectators. If your program or event has a headquarters, designate a central location to post updated brackets along with other important information.

Your response: _____

_____

_____

_____

Start date: _____   Complete date: _____

8. FACILITIES PLANNING

This section concerns facilities management for the event you are planning and is not intended as a comprehensive guide to designing or managing facilities. Good planning of facilities is essential to running a successful event. Following the steps listed here will decrease the likelihood of your forgetting an important aspect of facility management for your event.

A. Determine your facility needs.

Your facility needs involve not only playing facilities but also locker rooms, restrooms, spectator seating, parking, traffic flow, and food service. Think about your needs for special lighting, temperature control, scoreboards, and timing systems. Is the facility accessible to the physically challenged, including doorways, restrooms, and spectator areas? You should also plan for many alternative facilities in case of bad weather. If you expect spectators, you need to plan for (a) sufficient access and exits to the site, (b) restroom facilities, (c) ticket taking if admission is to be charged, (d) procedures for cancellations and postponements, (e) means of dealing with disorderly people, and (f) plans for evacuation in case of emergency.

Your response: _____

_____

_____

_____

Start date: _____ Complete date: _____

B. Reserve the facility.

Reserve the facility if you control it, making certain there are no schedule conflicts. If you do not control the facility, seek permission to use it by contracting with the controlling agency. Be sure you get an agreement in writing so that you are assured of having the rights to use the facility for the dates desired. The Facility Rental Agreement should also specify clearly what parts of the facility are included or excluded (such as the locker rooms, toilets, and food service areas), who will be responsible for supervising and maintaining the facility, what compensation, if any, is required for the use of the facility, and whether liability and insurance issues exist. A sample Facility Rental Agreement is provided in Form 11 on page 78.

Your response: _____

_____

_____

Start date: _____ Complete date: _____

C. Determine who will supervise the facility.

If you are responsible for the facility, it is your duty to assign and properly train a supervisor. If you rent the facility from another agency, the agency may stipulate that it will provide a certain level of supervision and maintenance, or it may pass that responsibility on to you. If it is your responsibility, you will want to assign supervisors to each facility for the duration of the event. Be sure that the supervisor addresses the issue of locker room security while participants are involved in events.

Your response: _____

_____

_____

_____

Start date: _____   Complete date: _____

D. Arrange for access to the facility.

If you are renting the facility and supervision is provided by the rental agency, you need to coordinate with the supervisor access to the facility at the appropriate times. If you are responsible for supervising the facility, you need to be sure you have all the keys you need, including keys to buildings; gates; equipment storage areas; locker rooms; toilets; and lighting, sound, and temperature control panels.

Your response: _____

_____

_____

_____

Start date: _____   Complete date: _____

E. Prepare the facility prior to the event.

Prior to the event determine if you need to do any of these tasks:

- Clean the facility and schedule for cleaning during the event (sweeping and mopping floors, etc.).
- Modify the facility for the event.
- Eliminate or reduce any hazards you find as a result of your risk analysis.
- Prepare the playing area (cut the grass, mark the field, paint lines, erect nets, etc.).
- Prepare the spectator area.
- Prepare the locker rooms or other dressing accommodations.
- Prepare the scorer's and timer's areas.
- Make arrangements for the officials' area.
- Prepare signs to direct people.

- Prepare the sound and lighting systems.
- Prepare restrooms for participants, other personnel, and spectators.
- Make certain the facility has adequate water supplies for drinking and maintenance.

Your response: _____

_____

_____

_____

Start date: _____   Complete date: _____

F. Arrange for maintenance of the facility.

Depending on the sport, a great deal of maintenance may be involved for the event. If maintenance is your responsibility, consider these steps:

- Determine who will be responsible for maintenance.
- Develop and use a facility inspection schedule. All indoor facilities should be inspected on a daily basis. For outdoor facilities, perform an inspection two to four months before the start of the season so there is time to correct any problems or to complete any upgrades. Once the season starts, site supervisors should perform a daily inspection and report any problems to the agency. These facilities should be inspected before and after contests. Use Form 12 on page 80 to develop a checklist specific for your facilities.
- Decide the maintenance schedule for the playing area during and after the event.
- Establish the maintenance schedule for other facilities such as the locker room, toilets, and spectator area.

Your response: _____

_____

_____

_____

Start date: _____   Complete date: _____

G. Arrange for security for all facilities.

Security will most likely be the responsibility of the supervisor of the facility, but if it is not, make sure that someone is assigned to securing all parts of the facility.

Your response: _____

_____

_____

_____

Start date: _____   Complete date: _____

H. Arrange for adequate parking if needed.

Determine how much parking is needed, if reserved areas are required, if directional signs or attendants to direct parking are needed, and if security for vehicles is required. For larger events, consider requesting traffic police.

Your response: _____

_____

_____

_____

Start date: _____   Complete date: _____

9. EQUIPMENT, UNIFORMS, AND SUPPLIES PLANNING

Sometimes you will be responsible for providing playing equipment, uniforms, and other supplies needed for your event. If it is the responsibility of the players or their parents to purchase some equipment (e.g., tennis racquets, softball/baseball gloves), recommend to them what items need to be purchased, what quality is appropriate, what price range is acceptable, and where the items can be purchased. When you are responsible for equipment, uniforms, and supplies for the event, the following steps should help you. If the event is large, consider having a playing equipment committee to oversee all aspects of this category.

A. Inventory what is available.

Know what you have by taking inventory and determining its condition. See Forms 13a and 13b on pages 84 and 85 for two kinds of simple inventory forms that you can use or adapt. You will need to inventory supplies regularly because these are consumables.

Your response: _____

_____

_____

_____

Start date: _____   Complete date: _____

B. Determine what is needed for the event.

Calculate what your need will be based on the number of participants (and records of previous events, if available) and subtract what you have on hand to determine what you need to purchase. Consider having extras available during the event so there will be virtually no chance of running out.

Your response: _____

_____

_____

_____

Start date: _____   Complete date: _____

C. Purchase what is needed.

If you permit others to make purchases for the event, then you'll need to develop a system for controlling these purchases. Otherwise the amount spent may exceed your budget, and the type of equipment and supplies bought may not meet your requirements. If you are making the purchases, consider these guidelines:

- Know what you are purchasing. Do the necessary research to become educated about the equipment.
- Purchase from reputable dealers who will stand behind their product. Specify the turnaround time you need and be sure the vendor can meet your time frame.
- Compare prices among dealers or bid out the purchase.
- Make certain the equipment meets the recommended safety standards.
- Purchase the best quality and durability you can afford.
- Purchase in quantity to get better prices.
- See if you can return unused inventory.
- Find out if you can purchase additional equipment and supplies quickly if you run out during an event.

Your response: _____

_____

_____

_____

Start date: _____   Complete date: _____

D. Inventory new purchases.

Make certain that you received the quantity and style that you ordered. Mark each uniform and piece of equipment to identify it for inventory. Identify your organization, the unit number, date of purchase, serial number, size, and so on, as appropriate for the item.

Your response: _____

_____

_____

_____

Start date: _____   Complete date: _____

E. Distribute the equipment, uniforms, and supplies.

Create procedures for distributing and collecting these items. Keep a record of where all equipment is located, who has uniforms, and where supplies are distributed. Have players sign out equipment, acknowledging that they've received items in good condition and will return them in similar condition after the event/season. Form 14 on page 86 is a sample equipment distribution form. Feel free to use or adapt it—you may want to develop sport-specific forms.

Your response: _____

_____

_____

_____

Start date: _____   Complete date: _____

F. Plan for storage and security.

Develop plans for short-term storage of equipment, uniforms, and supplies so that they can be readily accessed by those with permission to do so. Develop plans for the long-term storage of these items during the off-season. Give careful consideration to the security of these items during their short- and long-term storage.

Your response: _____

_____

_____

_____

Start date: _____   Complete date: _____

G. Inspect and maintain the equipment.

As part of your risk management plan, the equipment should be inspected regularly (you can combine this inspection with your inventory check). Use (or modify) Form 15 on page 87 to conduct your equipment inspection. When equipment is found to be damaged, write down the item, location, and if it should be repaired or replaced. Proper maintenance of equipment will reduce the risk of injury and extend the life of the equipment.

Your response: _____

_____

_____

_____

Start date: _____   Complete date: _____

10. AWARDS AND RECOGNITION PLANS

Everyone likes to be recognized for their accomplishments, yet it is important that awards and recognition are appropriate in sports programs. As you plan your event, decide what types (if any) of awards and recognition you want to offer to the players, teams, coaches, and other helpers. What types of awards are appropriate for the level of competition? As you plan for awards and recognition, think carefully about the contribution of these awards and recognition to your program objectives. If the event is large, consider developing an awards committee to be responsible for the tasks in this category.

A. Determine for what achievements awards will be given and how they will be given.

For your event, what types of awards are appropriate? Consider awards for participating, sportsmanship, and achievement in sport. Will you give awards to those who place first, second, third, and so on? Do you give awards to recognize teams only or individuals too? What criteria should you use for selecting individuals or teams to receive awards? How can you make the selection as fair as possible? Establish these criteria before the event, and inform participants of awards to be given during the event.

Your response: _____

_____

_____

_____

Start date: _____   Complete date: _____

B. Determine the types of awards to be given.

First decide how much money to spend on the awards. This decision should be based on your overall budget. Then select the type of award from such items as trophies, medals, plaques, ribbons, certificates, pins, T-shirts, hats, jackets, sports equipment, and photographs. Be sure that no awards will jeopardize any athlete's amateur status. If you have any questions regarding this, check with your state's activities/athletic association or the national governing body for the sport.

Your response: _____

_____

_____

_____

Start date: _____   Complete date: _____

C. Purchase the awards.

Get bids from vendors who will provide you with the product and service you need for your awards. Consider not only the price and quality but also the reliability of the vendor delivering what you need on time.

Your response: _____

_____

_____

_____

Start date: _____   Complete date: _____

D. Plan for the storage of the awards before the event.

Keep the awards properly stored and secure. Some awards require considerable space and because of their value need to be kept under lock and key.

Your response: _____

_____

_____

_____

Start date: _____   Complete date: _____

E. Plan for the display of the awards during the event.

Often awards are displayed during the event for participants and spectators to view. You should decide if you wish to do this and, if so, how to prevent the awards from being stolen or vandalized.

Your response: _____

_____

_____

_____

Start date: _____   Complete date: _____

F. Plan for the presentation of awards.

If awards are to be given, give them with class. Determine what is the best time to give the awards, who will present the awards, what ceremony if any will accompany the award presentation, and what is to be said about the award and its recipient. Consider the need for a PA system. Determine if you want to send news releases to the media about the awards given.

Your response: _____

_____

_____

_____

Start date: _____   Complete date: _____

G. Plan for recognizing those who have contributed to the event in various ways and implement those plans.

It is valuable to recognize those who have contributed to making your event successful. Sponsors, coaches, officials, scorekeepers, timers, facility maintenance staff, and others who have helped put on the event should be considered for recognition. During the presentation of awards, you can recognize these contributors with a verbal thank you. You can also list them in the tournament brochure and perhaps give them a commemorative souvenir, like a T-shirt or cap.

Your response: _____

_____

_____

_____

Start date: _____   Complete date: _____

11. FOOD SERVICE PLANS

Decide what food and drink service you want and need to provide. Of course you will need water for the participants and others, but what beyond that? The sale of food and drinks is one way to raise additional revenue, but doing this requires well-organized service, perhaps a contract with a professional concessionaire. If you get into selling foods, be aware of and in compliance with local health department regulations. Find out about any facility policy regarding having food and drink in gyms or other facilities (indoor and outdoor). Consider if a hospitality tent is needed. If you plan to have extensive food and drink service, you will want to delegate someone to oversee this function.

A. Arrange for drinks for participants.

Determine what your needs will be. They will vary depending on the temperature and the intensity of the activity. Consider these questions:

- Where will you get the water?
- How will it be stored?
- How will it be served safely and cost-effectively?

Your response: _____

_____

_____

_____

Start date: _____   Complete date: _____

B. Arrange for food for participants.

First determine what food you wish and need to make available to the participants. Then decide where the food will come from, how it will be stored, when it will be made available, and how it will be served.

Your response: _____

_____

_____

_____

Start date: _____   Complete date: _____

C. Arrange for refreshments for other personnel.

Answer the same questions for other personnel as you have for the participants. What food and drink will you provide, where will it come from, how will it be stored, when will it be dispensed, and how will it be served? Consider having a hospitality room.

Your response: _____

_____

_____

_____

Start date: _____   Complete date: _____

D. Arrange for refreshments for spectators.

Determine what service you wish to provide parents and other spectators. Consider if a concessionaire should handle this service, freeing you from managing another item.

Your response: _____

_____

_____

_____

Start date: _____   Complete date: _____

E. Determine whether a hospitality room is needed.

For some events, you may wish to have a hospitality room for participants, coaches, workers, supporters, and the media. If you have a hospitality room, consider staffing needs, the possibility of obtaining food and beverage donations, and the potential for additional advertising.

Your response: _____

_____

_____

_____

Start date: _____   Complete date: _____

12. TRANSPORTATION PLANS

Virtually all club and interscholastic sport seasons involve traveling to other competition sites (either in your city or out of town). Careful consideration must be given to methods and legal liability issues involved in transporting athletes and other participants.

A. Determine what transportation is needed.

You must first decide if you need to offer transportation for the event or if it is the responsibility of the participants. If the event involves traveling to another city, you will need to coordinate travel plans for the team or group. If the event brings a number of teams into your city, you may need to plan transportation from hotels to the playing sites. If the event involves multiple sites, consider how players will travel from site to site. You also need to think about the transportation needs of officials and others helping to conduct the event.

Your response: _____

_____

_____

_____

Start date: _____   Complete date: _____

B. Communicate what transportation will be offered.

When you determine the type of transportation you will provide, you will need to inform those to be transported how the service will work. When is the transportation provided? How often will vehicles run? From where will vehicles depart? Will the vehicles have room for equipment and baggage? How many people can travel in a vehicle at once? Is the vehicle wheelchair accessible? If teams are traveling from out of town, they will want to know all the details about transportation. Make sure transportation details are included in the information sent to the team prior to their arrival. Have signs made and placed where transportation information may be needed.

Your response: _____

_____

_____

_____

Start date: _____   Complete date: _____

C. Arrange for the vehicles to provide the transportation.

If using school or commercial transportation, reserve the vehicles needed. Do you also need to secure a driver, or can the coach drive the vehicle? For liability reasons, be sure to obtain proof of insurance for *all* drivers. We strongly caution against the use of student drivers. If you'll be using public transportation, you'll need to contract for it. Make sure that transportation agreements are in writing, all insurance and liability issues have been covered, and you understand the responsibilities of using the vehicle (e.g., leaving it free of garbage, full tank of gas, etc.).

Your response: _____

_____

_____

_____

Start date: _____   Complete date: _____

13. HOUSING PLANS

Planning for housing becomes necessary when teams travel out of town and participate in events lasting more than one day. You will need to consider whether you will use a hotel or motel, or a special facility such as a university dormitory. Some event directors choose to provide private housing to accommodate visiting teams, particularly club sport directors and directors of individual sporting events. If you will have extensive housing requirements, assign someone to coordinate housing.

A. Determine the need and cost of housing for participants, officials, and others.

The first step is to evaluate whether housing is needed and, if so, for whom. If it is needed, what is the extent of the need and the best way to accommodate people? Keep expense and safety in mind.

Your response: _____

_____

_____

_____

Start date: _____   Complete date: _____

B. Arrange for the accommodations.

Make reservations with hotels and motels, contract with other special housing units, or make sure you have commitments from the parents of home players to house the visiting players. Try to negotiate special room rates at a hotel or motel. Obtain addresses and telephone numbers of the places where players will be housed so they can be contacted easily. When staying at hotels/motels, consider having long distance phone calls and movie channels blocked. Determine if check-out times correspond to event times, and whether the hotel/motel can offer an extended check-out time.

Your response: _____

_____

_____

_____

Start date: _____   Complete date: _____

C. Communicate what will be offered.

Remember to inform those involved well in advance so they can plan for their stay. Let people know what type of housing is available, how much it will cost, and if they'll need to bring towels or other items.

Your response: _____

_____

_____

_____

Start date: _____   Complete date: _____

D. Set up a housing registration system.

If you are coordinating housing for large numbers of participants coming to a site, you will need a system to register guests, to assign housing, and to provide participants with the information they need to find the place they are staying. Do as much of this preparation as possible prior to the visitors' arrival.

Your response: _____

_____

_____

_____

Start date: _____   Complete date: _____

E. Set up a system to supervise housing.

If athletes are not supervised, you may need to arrange supervision for them while they are being housed, especially if they are staying in dormitory-type living quarters. Consider offering some special events for nonparticipating attendees.

Your response: _____

_____

_____

_____

Start date: _____   Complete date: _____

14. PROMOTION PLANS

Effective promotion has several components. First, you want to let your target audience know about your event. Then, you want to encourage them to either participate or attend. Determining who, what, and how are all important aspects of effectively promoting your event. The following tasks will help you develop your promotion plans.

A. Determine what you want to promote and to whom.

You may be promoting a new league that needs players, or you may be promoting a tournament that needs the participation of existing teams from other schools or clubs. In high school and club team sports programs you usually do one or more of the following:

1. Promote the event to the students/individuals for whom you have planned the event.

2. Promote the event to opposing teams who you want to participate in the event.

3. Promote the event to coaches, officials, and other volunteers who might help you conduct the event.

4. Promote the event to potential spectators, including parents, who you hope will come watch the event.

5. Promote the event to potential sponsors.

6. Promote the event in your community or many communities.

Your response: _____

_____

_____

_____

Start date: _____   Complete date: _____

B. Determine how the event will be promoted to participants.

Select from this list the methods you will use to promote the event to the audience you've chosen.

1. Advertising (promotions that cost you money to deliver the message)

   • Newspaper and newsletter advertising

   • Radio and television advertising

   • Magazine advertising

   • Brochures and flyers mailed directly to your audience, including all the previous year's participants

   • Billboards

2. Publicity (basically, free advertising)

- Announcements during homeroom meetings in schools
- Press or news releases for newspapers, radio, and television
- Interviews on radio and television talk shows
- Public service announcements in newspapers, radio, and television
- A press briefing for the media immediately before the event
- Flyers and brochures distributed door-to-door and through retail outlets and various public agencies
- Posters placed in prominent locations in schools, retail outlets, and other public places

3. Personal contact

- Speaking at places where the audience meets (e.g., schools, service clubs, professional societies)
- Initiating telephone contact
- Asking current participants to contact a certain number of people directly

4. Special methods

- Advertising a door prize to be given away during event, but winner must be present
- Piggybacking your message with advertising and promotion by others or mailings done for another purpose (e.g., insert your message in the local cable TV monthly statements)
- Promoting the event at local exhibits, fairs, and displays
- Asking organizers of other events with the same target audience if you can stuff a flyer in their registration packets
- Attending similar events and hand distributing information about your event or placing flyers on car windshields

Your response: _____

_____

_____

_____

Start date: _____   Complete date: _____

C. Prepare the promotional materials.

Whether the promotional material is an advertisement, press release, poster, or brochure, it should be prepared as professionally as possible for the budget available. A very poorly prepared promotional piece will have adverse effects on the image of your event and program. For interscholastic and club league play, consider promoting your event through schedule cards and posters distributed throughout your community (you can pay for these by selling advertising space). A sample press release promoting an event and a sample schedule card follow.

Your response: _____

_____

_____

_____

Start date: _____   Complete date: _____

Sample Press Release

Lincoln Senior High School
312 E. 32nd Street
Bloom Hills, IL 61821

Sioux Valley Conference
Girls Basketball Conference Tournament

For Immediate Release
Friday, March 17, 1996

Contact: Kent Houston
Lincoln Patriot Athletic Department
338-4451

Bloom Hills—Friday, March 10, and Saturday, March 11, at the Lincoln Senior High School gym, teams from Lincoln, Washington, Lakewood, and East will compete for the Sioux Valley Conference basketball title. Lincoln is the pretournament favorite.

Games on Friday match East against Washington at 6:00 p.m., followed by Lakewood and Lincoln at 8:30 p.m. The losers of these two games will compete for third place on Saturday at 3:00 p.m., with the championship game following at 5:30 p.m. The winner of the Sioux Valley Conference Tournament is assured a berth in the state tournament to be played March 17 through 19.

Attendance fees for high school students and younger are $4.00 per day, while adult attendance fees are $6.00 per day. Two-day passes are available for $6.00 and $8.00, respectively. For more information, please call Kent Houston at 338-4451.

				199_ Your Organization Name Sports Schedule
	AD		AD	

				FULL PANEL AD
	AD		AD	

D. Release the promotional materials.

The key to effective promotion is releasing the materials at the right time. You want to release neither too early nor too late. Timing is important, and you'll need to determine what is best for your event and the method of promotion you are using. Be sure to let the paper and radio know how long to promote your event.

Your response: _____

_____

_____

Start date: _____   Complete date: _____

E. Plan for responding to the inquiries generated by the promotion.

On occasion, individuals have promoted an event without preparing to respond to the inquiries generated by the promotion. Are people to respond by telephoning, mailing in a response, or coming in person? Does the director of the event need to finalize all registrations and their acceptance? Do you have sufficient staff to respond to the anticipated response? Be sure your office staff is adequately informed about the event so they can answer any questions. If the expected audience response is to register to participate in the program, you may have planned for this in the registration plan described earlier (Category 6. Registration Plans).

Your response: _____

_____

_____

Start date: _____   Complete date: _____

15. PUBLIC RELATIONS PLANS

Public relations is managing the image of your athletic program and the event you are conducting. It is especially important that you address public relations for events in which you want the teams, players, parents, coaches, and other volunteers to participate again. The key to good public relations in high school sports programs is serving participant needs and interests well. For a large event, consider developing a media and public relations committee to oversee and manage all aspects of this category.

A. Plan your PR with parents.

An important aspect of PR with parents is communicating with them about their daughter's or son's participation in your event. Let them know about the steps you'll take to ensure the safety of all involved. If parents must register their children for the event, handling the registration process with friendly, efficient service will go a long way toward building PR with parents. Develop a system for responding promptly to and documenting complaints. For league participation, a preseason parent-athlete meeting is a good opportunity to initiate PR with parents. See the following information about the sport director's role and possible agenda items.

Your response: _____

_____

_____

_____

Start date: _____   Complete date: _____

Preseason Parent Meeting

A preseason parent meeting is a good opportunity for you, the sport director, to meet the parents of the athletes in your program. Parents will appreciate the opportunity to meet you and to know that you're willing to discuss your program and their child's participation in it at anytime. Some possible agenda items include

- coach and staff introductions;
- program philosophy, goals, and objectives;
- parental involvement and support;
- athlete expectations; and
- athlete team member policies.

B. Plan your PR with coaches, officials, and other volunteer help.

The most important aspect of PR with coaches, officials, and other volunteers is keeping them informed about developments that affect them. Most people do not respond well when they are surprised to learn about changes in an event. When possible, it's also a good idea to give volunteers the opportunity to offer their input during meetings prior to the event.

Your response: _____

_____

_____

_____

Start date: _____   Complete date: _____

C. Plan your PR with the media.

Invite the media to a news briefing before the event, accommodate them at the event, and be sure to follow up by providing them with the results after the event. Invite sponsors and/or community leaders to the event to talk to the media also. Having a hospitality tent or room with refreshments where media and other VIPs can congregate is a great way to accommodate them.

Your response: _____

_____

_____

_____

Start date: _____   Complete date: _____

D. Prepare your paid staff and volunteers to be good ambassadors for your event and agency by encouraging them to be courteous and helpful.

In your written and oral communications with your staff, express your desire to make the event a positive experience for all involved. Describe how you would like them to handle problems and complaints so that participants feel satisfied. Role playing certain situations can be a good way to prepare staff for interaction with the public. When placing staff, consider putting your most courteous and friendly personnel in the most visible places.

Your response: _____

_____

_____

_____

Start date: _____   Complete date: _____

16. COMMUNICATION PLANS

So often we see technically well-organized events break down because of communication problems. Don't assume anything with communication—others can't read your mind. In developing your event plans, don't forget the importance of good communication among yourself, your staff, your participants, and others.

A. Develop a communication system between you and your directors and your directors and their staff.

Consider pre-event, event, and postevent communication. How will you communicate with staff during the event, especially if you use multiple sites or hold multiple contests within a large site? How will changes and updates be announced? Will you have a message center? Will you need runners, phones, voice mail or voice tel, and so on? If you are using multiple sites, remember you will have to plan for communication among the sites. Beepers, cellular phones, and walkie-talkies are quick and excellent ways to bridge distance, especially in emergency situations.

Your response: _____

_____

_____

_____

Start date: _____   Complete date: _____

B. Plan how to communicate with participants and coaches.

Keep participants and coaches informed about contest times, location, opponents, contest results, accommodations, food, lockers, mailings, and other details. This can be done via PA announcements, a tournament desk, or bulletin or other information boards.

Your response: _____

_____

_____

_____

Start date: _____   Complete date: _____

C. Plan a system for communication with spectators.

Plan introductions of players, officials, and coaches. Determine if you will need a PA system, scoreboards, and/or signs. Decide if you need to publish an event program. If so, you'll need to determine what the content will be and how it will be produced, paid for, and distributed.

Your response: _____

_____

_____

_____

Start date: _____   Complete date: _____

D. Plan a system for communicating with the media.

Delegate a person to keep the media informed prior to, during, and after the event. Press releases sent out before the event will prepare the media to schedule your event for coverage.

Your response: _____

_____

_____

_____

Start date: _____   Complete date: _____

E. Plan for communicating results to the high school activities/athletic organization or the governing body of the sport.

If your event is sanctioned, the activities/athletic organization or governing body needs to know the results of the event. Be certain you have the proper forms and know to whom and by when these results must be reported.

Your response: _____

_____

_____

_____

Start date: _____   Complete date: _____

17. EVENT EVALUATION PLAN

Once the event is over, it's still not quite over. A brief evaluation of the event will let you know what worked well and not so well so that you can improve on your next event. If you discover any items that we didn't think to include in this guide, add them to it and let us know so we can improve this tool for all athletic administrators and club team directors.

A. Determine the system for evaluation.

You can keep the evaluation informal by simply asking various people how well organized the event was and if they saw ways to improve it. Consider conducting a debriefing meeting with key personnel after the event. Also consider collecting information systematically, using a brief questionnaire to assess how coaches, officials, parents, staff, and volunteer helpers viewed the event. This strategy can be very beneficial since you're obtaining feedback from many different sources. But recognize that a potential downfall of written evaluations is a low return rate. Making the evaluation forms easy to complete and return will help increase the return rate.

Your response: _____

_____

_____

_____

Start date: _____   Complete date: _____

B. Prepare the evaluation questionnaire.

You'll need to prepare your own questionnaire to suit your specific event, but here are some typical questions to ask:

- How well organized was the event?
- Was the event adequately promoted?
- What aspects of the event could have been improved? How?
- What aspects of the event worked well?
- Was the event about the right length (or time, matches, games, etc.)?
- Were you kept adequately informed about the event? During the event?
- Were the facilities and equipment satisfactory?
- Will you plan to return next year? Why? Why not?

A brief sample evaluation form (Form 16) is included on page 91. Feel free to use or adapt it to fit your event.

Your response: _____

_____

_____

_____

Start date: _____   Complete date: _____

C. Have the evaluation forms completed by those selected to evaluate the event.

Determine the procedure you'll use to distribute the evaluation forms, and circulate them near the end of the event. If possible, request that evaluators return the questionnaires before leaving the event (otherwise you'll likely get a low response rate).

Your response: _____

_____

_____

_____

Start date: _____   Complete date: _____

D. Review and summarize the evaluation comments.

Collect the responses and review them with an open mind. Prepare a written critique of the event and share it with those who would benefit by reading it. Make note of what you believe are constructive criticisms and start thinking of ways to better manage those aspects of the event next time. Recognize that not all evaluations will contain constructive feedback: some will result from the nitpicky idiosyncrasies of a few individuals.

Your response: _____

_____

_____

_____

Start date: _____   Complete date: _____

18. STAFFING PLANS

A common mistake of less experienced athletic administrators and directors is failing to staff adequately and being reluctant to ask others for help, leaving an inordinate work load for themselves. The consequence often is that these directors are so busy performing various functions that they neglect their major responsibility—the coordinating and supervising of the other staff. If you are in charge of a large event, the importance of surrounding yourself with competent people cannot be underestimated because delegating responsibility is paramount to running this type of event. Recognize that staffing is not only recruiting the right people but also training, communicating with, motivating, supervising, evaluating, paying, and recognizing those who work with you to conduct the event.

A. Determine the staff required to conduct the event.

If you followed our directions in completing the Event Management guide, you have indicated who would be responsible for each of the tasks. This will make it much easier to determine all your staffing needs. Now review each category of steps and summarize your staffing needs using Form 3, Staff Planning Form, on page 59.

Your response: _____

_____

_____

_____

Start date: _____   Complete date: _____

B. Recruit the volunteers needed.

Even with superb planning, if you do not have good people to carry out the plans the event will be less than satisfactory. Develop a plan and time line for recruiting a pool of candidates to volunteer in areas that need help. Once you've obtained a pool, select and assign individuals to tasks. The information that follows provides a variety of audiences from which to recruit volunteers. With large events, the extra help of "floaters" is essential.

Your response: _____

_____

_____

_____

Start date: _____   Complete date: _____

Potential Sources for Volunteers

- Parents of program participants
- Nonparticipating athletes
- Members of school student-body
- Business women and men
- Professional groups such as doctors, lawyers, bankers, accountants, and so on
- College students and faculty, especially those in physical education
- Adult members of churches
- Military personnel living in the community
- Members of service clubs (Rotary, Lions, Optimists, Kiwanis, Moose, Elks, Civitans, etc.)
- Senior citizens' groups
- Teachers in local elementary and secondary schools
- Members of parent-teacher associations
- Local fitness/health club members
- Members of labor unions
- Adults who participate in local sports programs

C. Hire the employees needed.

Develop a plan and time line for hiring the employees required. Establish specific procedures regarding the hiring of these individuals (e.g., qualifications, payment procedures, expectations, etc.).

Your response: _____

_____

_____

_____

Start date: _____   Complete date: _____

D. Make assignments to all staff.

Appoint directors to head up the various committees you need such as finance, facilities, and promotion. Then, working with the director and select committee members, create job responsibility checklists for all personnel. These checklists can include schedules and time-tables of work to be completed. When determining job functions for the event, be sure to assign your top people to chair these functions.

Your response: _____

_____

_____

_____

Start date: _____   Complete date: _____

E. Provide orientation and training.

Determine who needs orientation and training and then provide it. Prepare written procedures for duties that the staff does not know, that are difficult to remember, and that are important to do correctly.

Your response: _____

_____

_____

_____

Start date: _____   Complete date: _____

F. Plan the communication system with staff.

Sustain a clear communication network before, during, and after the event; all involved should know to whom to talk about what. For large events, designate a continually staffed headquarters to serve as the hub of the communication network.

Your response: _____

_____

_____

_____

Start date: _____   Complete date: _____

G. Plan for supervision of staff.

A common mistake of inexperienced managers is to fail to supervise. Supervision is the essential step to insuring that your plans are followed by those to whom you have delegated responsibilities. Supervision is overseeing, guiding, and directing others as they perform their duties. It is not looking for mistakes or problems to criticize but seeking ways to facilitate staff to achieve the goal. Good supervision involves three steps:

1. Establishing clear expectations or standards regarding the duties assigned to a person.
2. Evaluating the person's performance against these standards.
3. Taking steps to correct performances that are not reaching these standards.

Your response: _____

_____

_____

_____

Start date: _____   Complete date: _____

H. Plan for the payment and/or recognition of your staff.

Prompt payment of hired personnel is very important; thus be sure to pay temporary employees by the time you've agreed upon. Officials often expect to be given a check immediately before or after the event. Make plans to recognize volunteers (publicly if possible) for their contributions. Some ways to recognize staff and volunteers include giving them T-shirts or hats that show they are involved with the event, putting their names and photos in the program or on a bulletin board where the trophies are displayed, or having them step forward at an award ceremony. After the event, send thank you notes to all involved.

Your response: _____

_____

_____

_____

Start date: _____   Complete date: _____

CONDUCTING THE EVENT

Your event will now run perfectly because you have planned it perfectly, right? Don't count on it. Good planning is vital, but now you must see that the plans are carried out. You will find that not everything was planned as perfectly as you thought, and you will have to respond to problems—even crises—as they arise. Remember Murphy's law: "If it can go wrong, it will." It's normal to have problems when you are directing an event and you should be prepared for them both psychologically and situationally. You can be psychologically prepared by just expecting the "unexpected." To prepare yourself situationally, consider having a "trouble table" at the event to handle unforeseen situations. Another precaution is having extra floaters or troubleshooters to handle problems when they arise.

Once others join you in preparing for the event and helping you conduct it, your most important role is to provide leadership—directing and moving the team forward. You need to control events by monitoring and supervising others to be sure plans are carried out. You need to head up the communication system, making certain that everyone keeps informed. You need to be the inspiration and source of motivation for those who tire along the way. And for those problems that are yours as director, prepare yourself to resolve them as they arise—because they will arise. Expect, for instance, that some people to whom you have assigned tasks will let you down. Or an official or timer may not show up. You may run into inclement weather, throwing off your entire schedule. You may encounter facility or equipment problems. You may need to resolve a dispute or conflict among people. And almost certainly communications will break down here and there and the situation will need your attention. As the event gets underway, take the time to take copious notes of thoughts about improving the event or altering the way something was done. These can be used to improve future events, and by taking the time during the event you'll be assured of having this information long after the event is over.

As you provide the leadership and supervision required, remember why you are doing this: to help young people enjoy sports and benefit from what sports have to offer. Don't lose sight of the fact that the event should be fun for the players, coaches, parents, other people who help, and you!

 **Form 1**

EVENT PLANNING CHECKLIST

Use this form as you read through the Event Management guide. Consider each category and determine whether or not it applies to your event. Once you've determined this, put a check in the appropriate column. If you aren't sure, check the question mark column and come back to that category once you've gathered more information about your event. If you need more detail regarding a particular category or the tasks within, refer to the page reference where the category can be found. Use the extra spaces at the end of the form to add categories that we have not included (you may not realize what these categories are yet, so don't worry if you have to add them later).

Category	Yes	No	?
1. Planning the event objectives (pages 1–3)	√		
2. Financial planning (pages 4–7)			
3. Rules and officials plans (pages 8–10)			
4. Coach development plans (pages 11–13)			
5. Risk and emergency plans (pages 14–17)			
6. Registration plans (pages 18–19)			
7. Scheduling plans (pages 20–22)			
8. Facilities planning (pages 23–26)			
9. Equipment, uniforms, and supplies planning (pages 27–29)			
10. Awards and recognition plans (pages 30–32)			
11. Food service plans (pages 33–34)			
12. Transportation plans (pages 35–36)			
13. Housing plans (pages 37–38)			
14. Promotion plans (pages 39–42)			
15. Public relations plans (pages 43–44)			
16. Communication plans (pages 45–46)			
17. Event evaluation plan (pages 47–48)			
18. Staffing plans (pages 49–52)			
Additional categories			
19.			
20.			
21.			

 **Form 2**

FINANCIAL PLANNING FORM
Model for Interscholastic/Club Sport Budget

Use this form to develop a financial plan for your event. You'll look at sources of income and estimated expenditures and compare these figures for a total budget. Directions are included at the beginning of each section of the form. Notice that all sections have an **Actual** column and an **Over/under budget** column. After the event, complete the form by filling in these two columns, and then determining where you were actually over and under budget. Save this worksheet to help you in planning budgets for similar events in the future.

Part I   Sources of Income

In this section you'll determine your sources of income, distinguishing between committed funds (those you know are available to you) and potential funds (good prospects for funds not yet locked up). For each category of funds, calculate a total by adding the committed funds and potential funds for each category.

	Committed ($)	Potential ($)	Total ($)	Actual ($)	Over/under budget ($)
School district funds					
Federal and state grants					
Registration and entry fees					
Participation fees					
Admission fees					
User fees for facilities and equipment					
Concession sales					
Other sales					
Private gifts and donations					
Special event fundraising					
Commercial sponsorships					
Other _____					
Other _____					
Total income					
	A	B	C		

Part II Sources of Expenditures

In this section, estimate your expenses for conducting this event.

	Budget ($)	Actual ($)	Over/under budget ($)
Personnel expenses	_____	_____	_____

Subcategories may include full- and part-time employees, officials, coaches, and supervisors. You also will record your benefits expenses here.

Education and training expenses	_____	_____	_____

These expenses are not included in many club or interscholastic sport budgets, but they should be, just as they are in most companies now. Record here expenses for the education of coaches, parents, and your permanent staff.

Facility expenses	_____	_____	_____

Subcategories may include facility operating expenses, maintenance, rental payments, and utilities. This category of expense does not include capital expenses for building new facilities or remodeling.

Equipment and uniform expenses	_____	_____	_____

Each of these could be separate accounts, with purchasing and repair as subaccounts for equipment, and purchase and cleaning as subaccounts for uniforms. If you operate a multisport program, you could divide these accounts further by each sport.

Supplies expenses	_____	_____	_____

These may include office supplies, cleaning supplies, toiletries, and training room/first aid supplies.

Food service expenses	_____	_____	_____

If you provide food or drink without charge, you will need to track these expenses. If you sell food and drink, record the purchase cost of the items sold here.

Housing and transportation expenses	_____	_____	_____

When your event includes traveling to another city, or providing housing and/or transportation for teams coming to your event, record these expenses here.

Promotion and public relations expenses	_____	_____	_____

These are expenses associated with informing potential participants and volunteers about the events in your program.

Legal and accounting expenses	_____	_____	_____

This expense category is for any legal work you have done, such as facility leases, sponsorship agreements, review of waiver forms, and any formal litigation action. It is also where you record any expense associated with keeping these records.

Insurance expenses	_____	_____	_____

These expenses include a wide range of possible insurances you may wish to purchase depending on your situation.

	Budget ($)	Actual ($)	Over/under budget ($)
Publications expenses	_____	_____	_____

Record under this category your costs to prepare schedules, rules, policy manuals, programs, and other materials to communicate with your constituents.

Awards and recognition expenses	_____	_____	_____

Enter here the purchase cost of trophies, medals, ribbons, certificates, banquet meals, and other forms of recognizing participants and volunteers in the program.

Communication expenses	_____	_____	_____

Telephone and postage are the two major expenses here.

Other expenses	_____	_____	_____

Accommodates whatever doesn't fit into the preceding accounts.

Total expenditures	_____	_____	_____
	D		

Part III   Summary

In this section, you'll calculate the difference between the anticipated income and expenses. First you'll need to transfer some figures. The lines are labeled to assist you in doing this.

	Committed ($)	Potential ($)	Budget ($)	Actual ($)	Over/under budget ($)
Total income	_____	_____	_____	_____	_____
	A	B	C		
Total expenditures			_____	_____	_____
			D		
Net income/(loss)			_____	_____	_____

Compare the committed funds (A) to expenses (D) first. If these funds cover the expenses, then you have no financial worries. If the committed funds do not cover expenses, then determine if the committed and potential funds combined (C) cover your expenses (D). If they do not, you need to develop plans for reducing your expenses or increasing income. If the combination does cover your expenses, calculate the amount that comes from potential funds (B) and give careful thought to the probability of obtaining these funds. Continue revising your budget as you obtain more accurate information about available funds and actual expenses.

Form 3

STAFF PLANNING FORM

Keep this Staff Planning Form handy as you complete your event management plan. Review the list of positions—they correspond to the categories of the Event Management guide. Mark out those not needed for your event. On this form only enter the manager's name for each planning category and not the names of the support staff. We assume you will have only one manager for each category. Often the same person will be the manager for several categories. Indicate the number of support staff needed prior to the event and the number of work hours needed from each, as well as the number needed during the event and the number of work hours needed from each. Insert in the "Other" space position titles for additional personnel needed.

Position	Pre-event #	Pre-event Hours	Event #	Event Hours
Event director _____				
Event planning assistant	___	___	___	___
Clerical assistant	___	___	___	___
Computer assistant	___	___	___	___
Other _____	___	___	___	___
Other _____	___	___	___	___
Financial manager _____				
Fundraisers	___	___	___	___
Other _____	___	___	___	___
Other _____	___	___	___	___
Rules and officials manager _____				
Officials (umpires, referees)	___	___	___	___
Scorekeepers	___	___	___	___
Timers	___	___	___	___
Judges	___	___	___	___
Announcers	___	___	___	___
Other _____	___	___	___	___
Other _____	___	___	___	___
Coaching manager _____				
Coaches	___	___	___	___
Assistant coaches	___	___	___	___
Team statisticians	___	___	___	___
Other _____	___	___	___	___
Other _____	___	___	___	___

Position	Pre-event		Event	
	#	Hours	#	Hours
Risk manager _____				
Physicians	_____	_____	_____	_____
Trainers	_____	_____	_____	_____
Other _____	_____	_____	_____	_____
Other _____	_____	_____	_____	_____
Registration manager _____				
Registration clerks	_____	_____	_____	_____
Check-in manager	_____	_____	_____	_____
Other _____	_____	_____	_____	_____
Other _____	_____	_____	_____	_____
Scheduling manager _____				
Other _____	_____	_____	_____	_____
Other _____	_____	_____	_____	_____
Facility manager _____				
Facility supervisor	_____	_____	_____	_____
Facility maintenance workers	_____	_____	_____	_____
Technical assistants	_____	_____	_____	_____
Ticket takers	_____	_____	_____	_____
Ushers	_____	_____	_____	_____
Parking assistants	_____	_____	_____	_____
Other _____	_____	_____	_____	_____
Other _____	_____	_____	_____	_____
Event equipment manager _____				
Site equipment manager	_____	_____	_____	_____
Other _____	_____	_____	_____	_____
Other _____	_____	_____	_____	_____
Awards manager _____				
Awards presenters	_____	_____	_____	_____
Other _____	_____	_____	_____	_____
Other _____	_____	_____	_____	_____
Food manager _____				
Food preparers	_____	_____	_____	_____
Food sellers	_____	_____	_____	_____
Food cleanup workers	_____	_____	_____	_____
Other _____	_____	_____	_____	_____
Other _____	_____	_____	_____	_____

Position	Pre-event		Event	
	#	Hours	#	Hours
Transportation manager _____				
Drivers	___	___	___	___
Other _____	___	___	___	___
Other _____	___	___	___	___
Housing manager _____				
Other _____	___	___	___	___
Other _____	___	___	___	___
Promotion manager _____				
Merchandise seller	___	___	___	___
Other _____	___	___	___	___
Other _____	___	___	___	___
Public relations manager _____				
Photographer	___	___	___	___
Publications assistant (programs, brochures)	___	___	___	___
Other _____	___	___	___	___
Other _____	___	___	___	___
Communications manager _____				
Other _____	___	___	___	___
Other _____	___	___	___	___
Event evaluation manager _____				
Other _____	___	___	___	___
Other _____	___	___	___	___
Staffing manager _____				
Volunteer coordinator	___	___	___	___
Paid help coordinator	___	___	___	___
Gate help coordinator	___	___	___	___
Scorekeeper manager	___	___	___	___
Other _____	___	___	___	___
Other _____	___	___	___	___

Form 4

SAMPLE COACHING APPLICATION FORM

Name _____   Telephone: Home _____

Address _____   Business _____

_____   Sex: Male ☐   Female ☐

_____   Age _____

1. Circle the highest year you completed in school:

   Elementary   1   2   3   4   5   6   7   8

   High School   1   2   3   4

   College   1   2   3   4   5   6   7   8

2. Work history

Company	Position	Dates
_____	_____	_____
_____	_____	_____
_____	_____	_____

3. For which sport are you applying to coach? _____

   Note: The sport you have written in here will be referred to as *this sport* in the remainder of the questionnaire.

4. Why do you want to coach this sport? (Be specific.) _____

   _____

   _____

   _____

Coaching Background

5. Have you *played* this sport?   Yes ☐   No ☐   Number of years _____

6. What other sports have you played?

Sport	Age level	Number of years played
_____	_____	_____
_____	_____	_____
_____	_____	_____

7. Have you *coached* this sport?   Yes ☐   No ☐   Number of years _____

8. What other sports have you coached?

Sport	Sponsoring agency	Age level	Years coached
_____	_____	_____	_____
_____	_____	_____	_____
_____	_____	_____	_____

9. Have you had any formal training as a coach? Yes ☐ No ☐ If yes, please describe (for example, PE degree, coaching courses, clinics, etc.). _____

_____

_____

10. Describe any informal training that would help you coach (for example, reading books, watching sports, etc.). _____

_____

11. Have you ever been convicted of a felony? If so, please explain. _____

_____

12. Do you have any medical conditions that may affect your ability to coach?   Yes ☐   No ☐

13. Please rate your knowledge of the following topics with regard to this sport by circling the appropriate number.
    1 = I know very little about it.
    2 = I have reasonably good knowledge about it.
    3 = I know a great deal about it.

    1 2 3 • Skills and strategies of the sport   1 2 3 • Developing sportsmanship

    1 2 3 • Rules of the sport   1 2 3 • Communication skills

    1 2 3 • Organizing practices   1 2 3 • Warm-up and physical conditioning techniques

    1 2 3 • Equipment needs and specifications   1 2 3 • Working with parents

    1 2 3 • Injury prevention and treatment   1 2 3 • Principles for teaching sport skills

    1 2 3 • Legal duties   1 2 3 • Managing time

14. Please list the name, address, and telephone number (if available) of two persons who can attest to your coaching potential. One should be your most recent supervisor.

Name	Address	Telephone
_____	_____	_____
_____	_____	_____

By signing below I recognize that I may be subject to a criminal background check.

_____   _____
           Signature   Date

 **Form 5**

SAMPLE COACHING INTERVIEW FORM

Consider the questions in the four categories below when interviewing potential candidates for your coaching positions. Use these as introductory questions to get the candidate talking. Then listen carefully and ask appropriate follow-up questions. Modify the questions below based on information presented in the Sample Coaching Application Form.

Interviewer's Name _____   Applicant's Name _____

Date _____   Position _____

Motives for Volunteering to Coach

Why do you wish to coach? _____

_____

_____

What do you hope to gain personally from coaching? _____

_____

_____

How much time can you commit to coaching? _____

_____

_____

Knowledge of the Sport

How would you conduct a typical practice? _____

_____

_____

How familiar are you with the rules of this sport? _____

_____

_____

What do you think would be helpful for you to learn about the sport to improve your ability to coach it?

_____

_____

Knowledge of How to Work With Young People

How would you describe your coaching philosophy? _____

_____

_____

What do you consider the important differences in coaching this age group compared to adults? _____

_____

_____

_____

Have you had other experience teaching or directing young people? _____

_____

_____

_____

Character and Emotional Stability

On what basis will you judge yourself to have been a successful or unsuccessful coach? _____

_____

_____

How long have you held your present position of employment? _____

_____

_____

What behaviors in other people irritate you? _____

_____

_____

Other Questions Based on Coaching Application

_____

_____

_____

_____

_____

 **Form 6**

ASEP COACHING APPRAISAL FORM

Coach name _____   Sport _____

Team _____   League _____

Appraiser _____   Date _____

Observation during: Practice   Competition

Minutes observed _____

Circle only one response using the following rating system.

	Unsatisfactory	Needs improvement	Adequate	Good	Excellent
Knowledge					
Knowledge of the sport (rules, skills, strategies)	1	2	3	4	5
Teaching of skills	1	2	3	4	5
Correcting errors	1	2	3	4	5
Management					
Organization of activities	1	2	3	4	5
Use of time	1	2	3	4	5
Involvement of athletes	1	2	3	4	5
Communication					
Provides clear instructions	1	2	3	4	5
Listens to others	1	2	3	4	5
Uses appropriate language	1	2	3	4	5
Health					
Provides safe environment	1	2	3	4	5
Conditions athletes properly	1	2	3	4	5
Is sensitive to athlete's self-esteem and emotions	1	2	3	4	5
Self-Control					
Physical appearance	1	2	3	4	5
Control of emotions	1	2	3	4	5
Use of tobacco, alcohol, or other drugs	1	2	3	4	5

	Unsatisfactory	Needs improvement	Adequate	Good	Excellent
Relationships					
With athletes	1	2	3	4	5
With parents	1	2	3	4	5
With other coaches	1	2	3	4	5
With officials and directors	1	2	3	4	5
Motivation					
Motivates athletes appropriately	1	2	3	4	5
Shows enthusiasm for coaching	1	2	3	4	5
Coaching philosophy					
Appropriate perspective about winning and losing	1	2	3	4	5
Coaching style	1	2	3	4	5
Coaches to make sport fun to play	1	2	3	4	5
Overall rating of coach	**1**	**2**	**3**	**4**	**5**

Recommendations to coaching director:

_____

_____

_____

_____

_____

Form 7

DESIGNING YOUR RISK MANAGEMENT PLAN

Follow the steps of this exercise to create a risk management plan for your event. Take your time and be thorough about completing it. It could pay off by preventing an injury and/or a lawsuit.

Step 1.   The first thing you want to do is determine specific potential risks. The accompanying two checklists of general risks will serve as a starting point to help you identify possible risks. Use the first checklist, Checklist of Event Risks, if you are running an event such as a tournament, interclub, or interscholastic competition. If you are planning league play across the season, use the second checklist, the Checklist of General Risks in Sport.

Checklist of Event Risks

Identify the risks in conducting this event by answering Yes or No to the following questions:

Have you ensured . . .

	Yes	No
proper supervision in all areas utilized by the event?	❏	❏
a plan for occurrence of adverse weather conditions?	❏	❏
safety checks for playing areas?	❏	❏
checks for defective or unsafe equipment?	❏	❏
facility maintenance before and during event?	❏	❏
plans for emergencies affecting all in attendance (spectators, workers, participants)?	❏	❏
plans for attending to participants' first aid/medical emergencies?	❏	❏
injury report plans?	❏	❏
the attendance of appropriate medical personnel/supplies?	❏	❏
fair and equitable opportunities for all participants?	❏	❏
qualified officials and other event personnel?	❏	❏
proper spectator facilities?	❏	❏
protected areas for spectators?	❏	❏
a system for warning spectators of any possible risks?	❏	❏
proof of insurance for any drivers providing transportation?	❏	❏

Checklist of General Risks in Sport

Identify the general risks in your sport program by answering Yes or No to the following questions:

Do coaches . . .

	Yes	No
provide a safe environment for practice and contests?	☐	☐
teach skills in developmentally appropriate progressions?	☐	☐
provide appropriate supervision for activities?	☐	☐
warn players of inherent risks in the activity?	☐	☐
enforce the rules and regulations of the sport and your organization?	☐	☐
match and equate players fairly for practice and contests?	☐	☐
provide proper first aid when injuries occur?	☐	☐
keep records of injuries and other emergencies?	☐	☐
ensure the civil rights of all participants?	☐	☐
understand the difference between ordinary negligence and gross negligence?	☐	☐
know the signs and symptoms of possible child abuse?	☐	☐
know that by law they must report to the appropriate authorities any reason they have to believe any vulnerable individual is being abused or neglected?	☐	☐
know whether the immunity laws in your state protect them against ordinary negligence?	☐	☐
know if they are covered under your organization's insurance program?	☐	☐
have a plan for obtaining medical assistance?	☐	☐
submit reports on all injuries and accidents?	☐	☐
transport participants using their personal vehicles?	☐	☐

Do you . . .

	Yes	No
follow a formal procedure for selecting qualified staff, officials, and coaches to conduct the program?	☐	☐
ensure that your staff, officials, and coaches are appropriately educated to perform their duties?	☐	☐
monitor all aspects of the program appropriately, especially the competitive events and the facilities in which they occur?	☐	☐
keep up-to-date job descriptions that define the coaches' duties?	☐	☐
supervise, evaluate, and provide feedback to your coaches about how to perform their duties?	☐	☐
honor equal employment opportunity guidelines when hiring or terminating a coach?	☐	☐
follow ADA mandates that policies, procedures, and practices that discriminate against the disabled population be eliminated?	☐	☐

Do you . . .

	Yes	No
keep your risk management plan up-to-date?	☐	☐
ensure that you and your staff are knowledgeable about certain standards regarding sports facilities and equipment purchasing and maintenance?	☐	☐
keep up-to-date with health, physical education, and medical organizations that offer recommendations on safe practices in sport, recommended ages for participation, conditions that disqualify participants from participation, preparticipation physical examinations, strength and conditioning guidelines, and drug use?	☐	☐
receive periodicals that provide coverage of risk management issues?	☐	☐
educate your staff and coaches?	☐	☐
supervise all aspects of your program or assign others to provide general and specific supervision?	☐	☐
assign others to supervise a playing facility or special event only after making sure they are competent to plan for the activity?	☐	☐
ensure that your staff members follow guidelines and a checklist for supervising sports facilities?	☐	☐
keep up-to-date supervision guidelines for all your programs?	☐	☐
ensure that all staff members follow guidelines and use a checklist for supervising the use of sports equipment?	☐	☐
maintain a careful system of record keeping that could serve as legal documentation in case of a lawsuit?	☐	☐
ensure that the parents of the participants in your program assume risk by signing waivers/releases and consent forms?	☐	☐
ensure that your organization purchases all the types of insurance it needs for staff and coaches?	☐	☐
keep an up-to-date Emergency Medical Response Plan that you developed in consultation with a local physician, preferably a sports medicine specialist?	☐	☐
require all participants to provide you with a medical history?	☐	☐
require all participants to have a preparticipation physical examination to identify potential medical problems?	☐	☐
ensure that all participants fill out an emergency information card?	☐	☐
train your coaches and supervisors about what to do and what not to do when players are injured?	☐	☐
ensure that all athletes in your programs are transported by licensed commercial carriers?	☐	☐
ensure that athletes who are not transported this way are transported instead by vehicles of your agency?	☐	☐
ensure that all drivers of your agency's vehicles are qualified?	☐	☐
ensure that the vehicles are in good repair and properly insured?	☐	☐
keep up-to-date policies to ensure that all personnel and athletes in your program are afforded due process?	☐	☐

Step 2. List each risk in your program by describing it under the "Source of risk" heading on the following form. You are considering two major types of risk: risk to the well-being of your participants and spectators; and risk to you, your staff, and volunteers with regard to legal liability and thus financial loss.

Your Risk Management Plan

Source of risk:

_____

_____

Probability of occurrence:	Low	Moderate	High
Severity if it occurs:	Low	Moderate	High

Method to reduce risk:

_____

_____

_____

Source of risk:

_____

_____

Probability of occurrence:	Low	Moderate	High
Severity if it occurs:	Low	Moderate	High

Method to reduce risk:

_____

_____

_____

Source of risk:

_____

_____

Probability of occurrence:	Low	Moderate	High
Severity if it occurs:	Low	Moderate	High

Method to reduce risk:

_____

_____

_____

Source of risk:

_____

_____

Probability of occurrence:	Low	Moderate	High
Severity if it occurs:	Low	Moderate	High

Method to reduce risk:

_____

_____

_____

Step 3.   For each risk you listed on the "Source of risk" form, determine the probability of the risk occurring and circle "High," "Moderate," or "Low" on the form. You may want to obtain the opinion of others about the probability of the risk occurring if you have minimal experience.

Step 4.   Next, estimate the potential severity of this risk should it occur and indicate the degree of severity by circling "High," "Moderate," or "Low."

Step 5.   Now for the critical step: Can you best deal with this risk in some way by (a) avoiding the risk, (b) reducing the risk, or (c) transferring the risk? Write down in the space provided the actions you believe best in your situation.

Implement your recommendations to alleviate the risk, communicate the plan to alert all those who need to know, and continually monitor the plan to add items missed in your initial evaluation.

 **Form 8**

SAMPLE WAIVER/RELEASE FORM

Sample Waiver/Release Form for the Sport of _____
(fill in sport name)

I realize that _____ is a vigorous physical activity that
(name of sport)

involves <u>(characterize the elements of the activity: e.g., height, flight, and rotation; violent body contact; rapid directional change)</u> _____

_____

_____

_____

I understand that participation in _____ involves certain inherent risks and
(name of sport)

that regardless of the precautions taken by_____
(name of organization providing program)

or the participants, some injuries may occur. These injuries might include, but are not limited to,

1. *(Give examples, being sure to*

2. *include the most common and*

3. *most severe injuries, e.g., blindness,*

4. *quadriplegia, death.)*

These injuries may result from hazards such as

1. *(List circumstances that might bring about the types of injuries cited above.*

2. *Again, be sure to include the most common hazards, e.g., being struck by*

3. *a racquet or ball, making initial contact with head while blocking or tackling.)*

4.

The likelihood of such injuries may be lessened by adhering to the following safety rules:

1. *(List safety guidelines and rules created to help prevent the*

2. *likelihood of these injuries. If unsure, contact your state*

3. *activities association or the sport's national governing body*

4. *for recommendations.)*

5.

To properly protect my own safety and that of my fellow participants, I agree to follow these rules as well as any others that may be given by my (coach/officials/supervisor). Further, in recognition of the importance of shared responsibility for safety, I agree to immediately report any noted deviations from the safety rules as well as any observed hazardous conditions or equipment to my (coach/supervisor).

I further certify that my present level of physical condition is consistent with the demands of active participation in _____ . Following is a full and complete list of all of my

(name of sport)

known health conditions that might affect my ability to participate:

_____

_____

_____

_____

I have carefully read the foregoing document. I have had the opportunity to ask questions and have them answered. I am confident that I fully know, understand, and appreciate the risks involved in active participation in _____ .

(name of sport)

Having been informed of the above program to provide sport opportunities for girls and boys, I, the parent of the above-named registrant, do hereby give my approval of his/her participation in any and all of the activities during the current season. I assume all the risks and hazards incidental to the conduct of the activities, and I do further release, absolve, indemnify, and hold harmless the _____ , the organizers, sponsors, supervisors,

(name of group)

volunteers, and officials, any or all of them. In case of injury to my son/daughter, I hereby waive all claims against the organizers, the sponsors, or any of the supervisors appointed by them. I am voluntarily requesting permission for my son/daughter to participate.

_____   _____
(signature of parent or guardian)   *(date)*

 **Form 9**

SAMPLE EMERGENCY CARE AND TRANSPORTATION CONSENT FORM

As the parent or guardian, I do herewith authorize the treatment by a qualified and licensed medical doctor of the following minor in the event of a medical emergency that, in the opinion of the attending physician, may endanger his or her life, cause disfigurement, physical impairment, or undue discomfort if delayed. The authority is granted only after a reasonable effort has been made to reach me.

I, the undersigned, also give the minor permission to be transported by _____ as part of his/her participation in the _____ program, by whatever means of transportation the _____ deems appropriate.

Name of minor _____ Relationship _____

Dates when release is intended: _____

This release form is completed and signed of my own free will with the sole purpose of authorizing medical treatment under emergency circumstances in my absence.

Signed _____ Date _____
                (parent or legal guardian)

Address _____ Phone _____

Family physician _____ Phone _____

Other contact in case of emergency:

Name_____ Relationship _____ Phone _____

 **Form 10**

SAMPLE REGISTRATION/ENTRY FORM

Fill in all appropriate spaces. Missing information will delay your registration. Photocopy this form for additional registrations or pick up a blank form at any _____ registration office. **The reverse side must be signed before your registration can be processed. Please include proof of eligibility with mail-in registration.**

Family last name: _____

Street address: _____

City: _____   State: _____   Zip: _____

Work phone: _____   Home phone: _____

Class ID #	Program title	Fee	Participant's first and last name	Gender/ height/weight	Birth date

Total payment $ _____   (Do not send cash.)

Shirt size: _____

Does registrant require any special accommodations or assistance for enjoyment of the program? (circle)
        Yes   No

If yes, please describe: _____

Indicate choice of payment: Check: _____   Money order: _____

Bank charge (circle):   Visa   MasterCard

Cardholder #: _____

Expiration date: _____   Signature: _____

Important Information

The <u>name of organization</u> is committed to conducting its sport/extracurricular programs and activities in the safest manner possible and holds the safety of participants in the highest possible regard. Participants and parents registering their son/daughter in sport/extracurricular programs must recognize, however, that there is an inherent risk of injury when choosing to participate in sport/extracurricular activities. The <u>name of organization</u> continually strives to reduce such risks and insists that all participants follow safety rules and instructions designed to protect the participant's safety.

Please recognize that the <u>name of organization</u> *does not* carry medical accident insurance for injuries sustained in its programs. Please review your health insurance policy for coverage. It must be noted that absence of health insurance coverage *does not* make the <u>name of organization</u> automatically responsible for the payment of medical expenses.

Due to the difficulty and high cost of obtaining liability insurance, the agency providing liability coverage for the <u>name of organization</u> requires the execution of the following Waiver and Release of All Claims. Your cooperation is greatly appreciated.

Waiver and Release of All Claims

Please read this form carefully and be aware in registering your son/daughter for participation in the above program(s), you will be waiving and releasing all claims for injuries your son/daughter might sustain arising out of the above program(s).

I recognize and acknowledge that there are certain risks of physical injury to participants in the above program(s) and agree to assume the full risk of any injuries, damages, or loss regardless of severity that my son/daughter may sustain as a result of participating in any and all activities connected with or associated with such program(s).

I agree to waive and relinquish all claims my son/daughter may have as a result of participating in the program against the <u>name of organization</u> and its officers, agents, servants, and employees.

I do hereby fully release and discharge the <u>name of organization</u> and its officers, agents, servants, and employees from any and all claims from injuries, damage, or loss that my son/daughter may have or that may accrue to my son/daughter arising out of, connected with, or in any way associated with the activities of the program(s).

I further agree to indemnify and hold harmless and fend the <u>name of organization</u> and its officers, agents, servants, and employees from any and all claims resulting from injuries, damages, and losses sustained by my son/daughter arising out of, connected with, or in any way associated with the activities of the program(s).

In the event of an emergency, I authorize <u>name of organization</u> officials to secure from any licensed hospital, physician, and/or medical personnel any treatment deemed necessary for my son/daughter's immediate care and agree that I will be responsible for payment of all medical services rendered.

I have read and fully understand the above program details, Waiver and Release of All Claims, and permission to secure treatment.

_____   _____

Parent/guardian signature   Date

 **Form 11**

SAMPLE FACILITY RENTAL AGREEMENT

— Rental Agreement —

Your logo

address   city   state   zip   phone

Day and date of use

Day and date of use

Rental agreement for
Name
Organization
Address
City / State/ Zip
Day phone   Evening phone

Program description:

Special arrangements:

$ _____ $ _____   _____
      Fee   Damage deposit   Payment due date
   separate checks please

The undersigned agrees to use <u>name of organization</u> property with care. Any damage or loss during the specified rental time and attributed to the above group is the financial responsibility of the undersigned. Damage deposits are returned based on the postrental inspection cosigned by the renter and building opener. Payment must be received by the date indicated above or reservation will be released. No refunds for cancellations within 2 business days of rental date. The undersigned and the above-named organization agree to accept and comply with all of the terms, conditions, and requirements set forth on the back of this rental agreement form.

_____   _____
Renter's signature   Date

☐ _____ Building Supervisor   Building opener _____
☐ _____ Director of Recreation
☐ _____ Director of Operations Ledger acct. # _____
☐ _____ General Manager

Prepared by _____   Date _____

— Conditions of Rental Agreement —

1. The (controlling agency) may require a cash deposit or an indemnifying bond, with acceptable sureties in the amount determined by the General Manager to cover any loss, damage, expense, or litigation sustained because of the permit holder's activity. Generally this requirement would be in effect for activities with intense use.

2. The (controlling agency) or the General Manager may revoke any permit previously granted at any time if it is determined that the application for permit contained any misrepresentation or false statement, or that any condition set forth in the policies governing the permit requested is not being complied with, or that the safety of the participants in the activities of the applicant or other patrons of or visitors to the facility is endangered by the continuation of such activity.

3. (Controlling agency) will not be liable for any claims for injury or damages resulting from or arising out of the use of the facility or premises adjacent thereto and the renter agrees to indemnify the (controlling agency) and hold it harmless against any and all such claims, damages, losses, and expenses. If requested by the (controlling agency), the renter shall carry insurance against such claims and furnish the (controlling agency) with a certificate of insurance evidencing same.

4. Alcoholic beverages are not allowed on (controlling agency) property.

5. Smoking is not allowed inside (controlling agency) buildings.

6. Requests for special equipment or assistance including electricity must be reviewed with (controlling agency) staff at time of use request. The cost of any special assistance or equipment will be charged to the user and paid in advance.

7. Buildings will be opened at the hour specified in the application and groups will vacate the building at the hour designated on the application.

8. Groups are responsible to see that all activities are properly controlled and supervised. Adequate adult chaperones must be provided if group members are under 21 years of age.

9. Due to space limitations, there are no provisions to store items in (controlling agency) facilities.

10. A park use permit is required for any group of 25 or more and permit holder agrees to comply with City of _____ Noise Ordinance.

11. Permit holder agrees to properly dispose of all trash that results from their activities.

 **Form 12**

SAMPLE FACILITY INSPECTION CHECKLIST

This form is provided as a sample facility inspection checklist and is designed to help you develop a checklist specific for your facilities. This is an incomplete checklist.

Name of inspector _____

Date of inspection _____

Name and location of facility _____

_____

Facility Condition

Circle Y (yes) if the facility is in good condition and N (no) if it needs something done to make it acceptable. Fill in what needs to be done on the line to the right.

Gymnasium

Y   N   Floor (no water spots, buckling, loose sections) _____

Y   N   Walls (vandalism free) _____

Y   N   Lights (all functioning) _____

Y   N   Windows (secure) _____

Y   N   Roof (no adverse impact of weather) _____

Y   N   Stairs (well lighted) _____

Y   N   Bleachers (support structure sound) _____

Y   N   Exits (lights working) _____

Y   N   Basketball rims (level, securely attached) _____

Y   N   Basketball backboards (no cracks, clean) _____

Y   N   Mats (clean, properly stored, no defects) _____

Y   N   Uprights/projections _____

Y   N   Wall plugs (covered) _____

Y   N   Light switches (all functioning) _____

Y   N   Heating/cooling system (temperature control) _____

Y   N   Ducts, radiators, pipes _____

Y   N   Thermostats _____

Y   N   Fire alarms (regularly checked) _____

Y   N   Directions posted for evacuating the gym in case of fire _____

Y   N   Fire extinguishers (regularly checked) _____

Other (list) _____

Locker Room(s)

Y   N   Floor _____

Y   N   Walls _____

Y   N   Lights _____

Y   N   Windows _____

Y   N   Roof _____

Y   N   Showers _____

Y   N   Drains _____

Y   N   Benches _____

Y   N   Lockers _____

Y   N   Exits _____

Y   N   Water fountains _____

Y   N   Toilets _____

Y   N   Trainer's room _____

Other (list)   _____

_____

Field(s)/outside playing area

Surface

Y   N   Not too wet or too dry _____

Y   N   Grass length _____

Y   N   Free of debris _____

Y   N   Free of holes and bumps _____

Y   N   Free of protruding pipes, wires, lines _____

Y   N   Line markers _____

Stands

Y   N   Pitching mound _____

Y   N   Dugouts _____

Y   N   Warning track and fences _____

Y   N   Sidelines _____

Y   N   Sprinklers _____

Y   N   Garbage _____

Y   N   Security fences _____

Y   N   Water fountains _____

Y   N   Storage sheds _____

Concession area

Y   N   Electrical _____

Y   N   Heating/cooling systems _____

Other (list)   _____

_____

Pool

Y   N   Equipment in good repair _____

Y   N   Sanitary _____

Y   N   Slipperiness on decks and diving board controlled _____

Y   N   Chemicals safely stored _____

Y   N   Regulations and safety rules posted _____

Lighting—adequate visibility

Y   N   No glare _____

Y   N   Penetrates to bottom of pool _____

Y   N   Exit light in good repair _____

Y   N   Halls and locker rooms meet code requirements _____

Y   N   Light switches properly grounded _____

Y   N   Has emergency generator to back up regular power source _____

Exits—accessible, secure

Y   N   Adequate size, number _____

Y   N   Self-closing doors _____

Y   N   Self-locking doors _____

Y   N   Striker plates secure _____

Y   N   No obstacles or debris _____

Y   N   Office and storage rooms locked _____

Ring buoys

Y   N   20-inch diameter _____

Y   N   50-foot rope length _____

Reaching poles

Y   N   One each side _____

Y   N   12-foot length _____

Y   N   Metal stress _____

Y   N   Good repair _____

Guard chair(s)

Y   N   Unobstructed view _____

Y   N   Tall enough to see bottom of pool _____

Safety line at break point in the pool grade (deep end)

Y   N   Bright color floats _____

Y   N   3/4-inch rope _____

First aid kit

    Y   N   Inventoried and replenished regularly _____

Stretcher, two blankets, and spine board

    Y   N   Inventoried and in good repair _____

Emergency telephone lights and public address system

    Y   N   Accessible _____

    Y   N   Directions for use visibly posted _____

    Y   N   Powered by emergency generators as well as regular power system _____

    Y   N   Emergency numbers on telephone cradle or receiver_____

Emergency procedures

    Y   N   Sign posted in highly visible area_____

Track

Surface

    Y   N   Free of debris _____

    Y   N   Free of holes and bumps_____

    Y   N   Throwing circles _____

    Y   N   Fences _____

    Y   N   Water fountains_____

Other (list)   _____

_____

Recommendations/observations: _____

_____

_____

_____

_____

_____

_____

SAMPLE INVENTORY FORM A

Item	Description	1 Quantity in		2 Quantity out (issued)		3 Quantity deleted (poor condition)		4 Quantity ordered	Date ordered	Date received	New total (1 + 2 − 3 + 4)	Miscellaneous notes
		#	Date	#	Date	#	Date					
Soccer balls	Size 5 Mikasa	120	6/5	30	6/5	4	6/5	75	6/10	7/5	161	vendor info. P.O. # cost

 **Form 13b**

SAMPLE INVENTORY FORM B

Item: _Soccer balls   Size 5_

	Date: January	Date: June	Date: January	Date: June
Description	Size 5 Mikasa			
Quantity in	120			
Quantity out	38			
Quantity deleted	4			
Quantity ordered	10			
Date ordered	3/1			
Quantity received	10			
Date received	3/30			
New total	164			
Notes	Mikasa don't deflate quickly —use same brand for next season.			

Form 14

SAMPLE EQUIPMENT DISTRIBUTION FORM

Use or adapt this form to help you record equipment distribution. In the equipment column, indicate what equipment was checked out. In the next two columns, indicate the date it was checked out and the item number. In the condition section, indicate the condition of the equipment (average, good, or new), and get the player's initials. When the equipment is returned, record the date and get the player's initials.

Player: _____   Sport: _____

| Equipment | Date checked out | Item number | Condition | | | Player initial | Date returned | Player initial |
			Average	Good	New			

 **Form 15**

EQUIPMENT INSPECTION CHECKLIST

Name of inspector _____

Date of inspection _____

Circle Y (yes) if the equipment is in good condition and N (no) if it needs something done to make it acceptable. To the right note what needs to be done.

Football

Y N Helmets _____

Y N Mouth guards _____

Y N Jerseys _____

Y N Pants _____

Y N Shoulder pads _____

Y N Hip pads/girdles _____

Y N Thigh pads _____

Y N Elbow pads _____

Y N Hand pads _____

Y N Shoes/spikes _____

Y N Tackling sleds _____

Y N Footballs _____

Other (list)

_____

_____

Basketball

Y N Jerseys _____

Y N Shorts _____

Y N Shoes _____

Y N Mouth guards (optional) _____

Y N Eye guards/goggles (optional) _____

Y N Knee pads _____

Y N Elbow pads _____

Y N Basketballs _____

Other (list)

_____

_____

Wrestling

Y   N   Singlets _____

Y   N   Shoes _____

Y   N   Headgear _____

Other (list)

_____

_____

Baseball

Y   N   Jerseys _____

Y   N   Pants _____

Y   N   Sliding pants/pads _____

Y   N   Leggings _____

Y   N   Protective cups _____

Y   N   Mouth guards (optional) _____

Y   N   Eye guards/goggles (optional) _____

Y   N   Caps _____

Y   N   Cleats/shoes _____

Y   N   Baseballs _____

Y   N   Bats _____

Y   N   Batting gloves _____

Y   N   Bases _____

Y   N   Pitching machines _____

Y   N   Gloves _____

Other (list)

_____

_____

Softball

Y   N   Jerseys _____

Y   N   Pants/shorts _____

Y   N   Leggings _____

Y   N   Sliding pants/pads _____

Y   N   Protective cups _____

Y   N   Mouth guards (optional) _____

Y   N   Eye guards/goggles (optional) _____

Y N Caps _____

Y N Cleats/shoes _____

Y N Softballs _____

Y N Bats _____

Y N Batting gloves _____

Y N Bases _____

Y N Pitching machines _____

Y N Gloves _____

Other (list)

_____

_____

Tennis

Y N Shirts/jerseys _____

Y N Shorts/skirts _____

Y N Shoes _____

Y N Eye guards/goggles (optional) _____

Y N Racquets _____

Y N Tennis balls _____

Y N Ball machines _____

Other (list)

_____

_____

Volleyball

Y N Shirts/jerseys _____

Y N Shorts _____

Y N Shoes _____

Y N Mouth guards (optional) _____

Y N Eye guards/goggles (optional) _____

Y N Knee pads _____

Y N Elbow pads _____

Y N Volleyballs _____

Other (list)

_____

_____

Soccer

Y N Jerseys _____

Y N Shorts _____

Y N Shoes _____

Y N Mouth guards (optional) _____

Y N Eye guards/goggles (optional) _____

Y N Shin guards _____

Y N Soccer balls _____

Other (list)

_____

_____

Hockey

Y N Helmets/chin straps _____

Y N Mouth guards _____

Y N Jerseys _____

Y N Pants _____

Y N Protective cups/supporters _____

Y N Ankle guards _____

Y N Shoulder pads _____

Y N Suspenders/belts/garters _____

Y N Sticks _____

Y N Shin pads _____

Y N Thigh pads _____

Y N Elbow pads _____

Y N Gloves _____

Y N Socks _____

Y N Shorts/long underwear _____

Y N Skates _____

Y N Pucks/balls _____

Other (list)

_____

_____

 **Form 16**

SAMPLE EVENT EVALUATION FORM

Please complete the following evaluation and return it to us before leaving this event. Your comments will help us to improve future events. Thanks for your input!

Rate the quality of	Low				High
the overall event	1	2	3	4	5
competition	1	2	3	4	5
event organization	1	2	3	4	5
scheduling	1	2	3	4	5
event staff	1	2	3	4	5
parking	1	2	3	4	5
officiating	1	2	3	4	5
facilities	1	2	3	4	5
food and beverage service	1	2	3	4	5
transportation	1	2	3	4	5
housing	1	2	3	4	5
communication between staff and participants	1	2	3	4	5
communication between staff and spectators	1	2	3	4	5

Please use this space to provide any other feedback regarding this event.

Thanks for your input!

Appendix A
Event Management Sample

The following puts the Event Management for SportDirectors guide into action by using a hypothetical event—an end-of-season conference basketball tournament. The tournament is scheduled to take place on March 10 and 11 with four teams competing. The host school, Lincoln High School, was awarded the tournament in early January. The competing teams were identified following the last weekend of regular season conference play, March 3 and 4.

As you look through this example, you'll notice that several categories and tasks have been deleted. Form 1, Event Planning Checklist, was used to determine relevant categories, and the remaining categories were deleted. Unnecessary tasks within the relevant categories were then deleted as well. Thus, this Event Management sample contains only the categories and tasks that are needed for this event.

Forms referred to in the categories can be found beginning on page 114.

1. PLANNING THE EVENT OBJECTIVES

Complete the tasks below if you are responsible for determining the objectives of an event. The size of the event might lead you to form a committee to help you. A committee approach can assure you that the objectives identified are the most appropriate. Also, when establishing objectives, be sure to consider other factors that could impact your objectives, such as finances and facilities, for example. If the objectives of the event are already determined, record your interpretations of the objectives here and share them with those who decided the original objectives to be sure that you are in agreement. Share the objectives with those who help you conduct the event.

A. Determine the type of event.

Your response: *Each team will play two games, one Friday and one Saturday. The Saturday game match-ups will be determined by Friday game results, with the winners playing on Saturday for the conference championship and the losers playing for third place.*

B. Determine for whom the event is planned.

Your response: *This conference championship is for the top four basketball teams in the conference, as determined by regular season records.*

E. Determine the dates and duration of the event.

Your response: *The dates of this tournament are March 10 and 11.*

F. Determine the location(s) of the event.

Your response: *The location for this event will be the Lincoln Senior High School gymnasium.*

2. FINANCIAL PLANNING

Although money should not be the most important planning concern, finances play a major part in feasibility —they help determine the "parameters of the event." Thus, a preliminary financial plan is necessary at this stage because your budget will influence your subsequent planning. It's also important to think about equity and fairness when distributing finances. Then, as you plan the steps in the other categories, you can be more precise in your financial estimates, permitting you to refine your budget. If the event is large, consider either assigning or hiring a financial manager to assist you or developing a finance committee to oversee the financial aspects of this event. Extra unplanned expenses will always crop up. Consider establishing or utilizing an Emergency Fund or Administrative Account to meet these unexpected expenses during the event. Be able to justify your budgets to the public, since they are considered open information and can be reviewed under the Freedom of Information Act.

A. Prepare a budget for the event.

Your response: *Completed Form 2. Budget is acceptable.*

B. Develop plans to obtain all income and implement these plans.

Your response: *We will receive a $500 stipend from the conference office for hosting the tournament. Projected income from admission fees:*

100 adults/night × $5.00/night × 2 nights = $1000
150 students/night × $3.50/night × 2 nights = $1050
Total = $2050

Projected income from concession sales: $500

C. Keep accurate records.

Your response: *Assign Paula as Financial Manager to maintain records on and manage all income and expenses during the weekend of event. Record all income and obtain receipts for all expenditures. After event use Form 2 to evaluate and record actual income and expenses.*

3. RULES AND OFFICIALS PLANS

You will need to make decisions about the rules you will use to govern the event. These rules should cover participant eligibility, the playing of the contests, and managing disputes and unsportsmanlike behavior. You will also need to determine how to officiate the contests and what officials you will need (e.g., referees, scorekeepers, timers, judges, etc.). Commonly the person coordinating the officials is responsible for directing the rules planning. Having a tournament or event director make final decisions on rules disputes is a good idea.

D. Determine who will officiate the contests and secure their services.

Your response: *The conference office will provide all officials and cover their fees. Check with conference office for names and information if we haven't heard from them by March 3.*

Start date: *March 1*   Complete date: *March 3*

E. Determine what other officials you need (e.g., scorekeepers, timers, judges, and announcers) and plan to obtain their services.

Your response: *I need to obtain three scorekeepers. The conference office will hire broadcast announcers, but I need to obtain one in-house announcer (see Form 3 for staff planning needs). Expenses for scorekeepers and the announcer are noted in budget (Form 2).*

Start date: *February 1*   Complete date: *February 10*

F. Determine whether a pre-event coach and officials meeting is needed.

Your response: *Plan to hold coach and officials meeting two hours prior to first game. Secure meeting room for this meeting.*

Start date: *February 27*   Complete date: *March 3*

G. Determine the procedures to follow when a protest is made by a player, coach, or team official.

Your response: *Confirm conference office providing impartial committee on site in case of any disputes.*

Start date: *February 20*   Complete date: *February 24*

H. Determine the procedures to follow when participants, coaches, and/or spectators display unsportsmanlike behavior or engage in criminal acts.

Your response: *Secure and empower law enforcement personnel in attendance.*

Start date: *February 27*   Complete date: *February 28*

5. RISK AND EMERGENCY PLANS

It is a good idea to analyze risks and develop a plan for reducing the chance of injury to those participating in or attending the event. The steps you take to reduce the risk of harm will also reduce the likelihood of a lawsuit. As part of a risk plan, you need to plan for emergencies.

A. Prepare a risk management plan for this event.

Your response: *Complete risk management plan in Form 7. Based on completed form, address any major risk management concerns.*

Start date: *January 30*   Complete date: *February 3*

E. Determine if you will be in compliance with local fire and safety ordinances for this event.

Your response: *Follow regular fire and safety plans for basketball events.*

F. If food is to be sold, determine what steps are necessary for compliance with local or state food inspection laws.

Your response: *Follow regular food handling regulations for basketball events.*

G. Prepare an emergency plan for this event.

Your response: *Implement and follow regular emergency plan for this event. Make sure all know regular plan is in effect.*

H. Develop a plan for managing spectators if large numbers are expected.

Your response: *Organize spectator seating in gym for team support. Distribute to participating schools policies for visiting bands, as well as for poster decorations. Notify custodial staff of anticipated spectator numbers, so adequate restrooms and supplies are available.*

Start date: *March 5*   Complete date: *March 8*

6. REGISTRATION PLANS

Depending on the event, you will likely need to have a registration period to obtain eligible candidates or teams to participate. You need to plan this part of the event carefully so that you obtain all the information you need during registration and you make the registration process convenient for those participating and efficient for you.

B. Determine what information you need to get during registration.

Your response: *The conference office will take care of obtaining any information required. They'll provide us with complete rosters by March 6.*

7. SCHEDULING PLANS

This category of tasks involves not only the dates of the event but also the scheduling of practices and contests for participants. If facilities are at a premium, which they often are, you may need a system for scheduling practice times. If planning a season schedule, in each task that follows consider other activities that schedule the same playing and practice areas. You may want to develop a usage priority list based on which sports are in-season, but make sure you can justify this usage schedule as fair and equitable. For a "one-shot" event (competition completed over the course of a day or weekend), the scheduling of contests can involve such duties as making league round-robin schedules, double-elimination tournament brackets, pairings for a wrestling meet, and so on. Scheduling the contests may be simple or quite complex, depending on the event. A good reference on this subject is John Byl's *Organizing Successful Tournaments*, available from Human Kinetics, P.O. Box 5076, Champaign, IL 61825 (800-747-4457). This book will help you work through the mind-twisting combinations of tournament players and games. Chapters are devoted to five major tournament types—single elimination, multilevel, double elimination, round robin, and extended—and their variations.

A. Determine the facilities available and compute the maximum number of practices and contests that can be held.

Your response: *Facilities will not be a problem. Each team will get 1-1/2 hours of practice the day of the event. Practice times will be assigned after conference provides draw and game match-ups to us. Teams in first game will get earlier practice times, while teams in last game will get later practice times.*

B. Determine the time of day to schedule practices and contests.

Your response: *Friday game times: 6:00 p.m. and 8:30 p.m.; Saturday game times: 6:00 p.m. (consolation teams) and 8:30 p.m. (championship teams). Friday and Saturday practice times: 9:00 a.m., 11:00 a.m., 1:00 p.m., and 3:00 p.m.. The teams playing at 6:00 p.m. will practice at 9:00 a.m. and 11:00 a.m. (order determined by coin flip), and teams in 8:30 p.m. game will practice at 1:00 p.m. and 3:00 p.m. (also determined by coin flip).*

F.   Print and distribute the schedule.

Your response: *The conference office will print and distribute posters listing participating teams and game times. Once we receive these posters, we will distribute them to custodial staff for posting on school grounds, as well as to student boosters for posting around town.*

8. FACILITIES PLANNING

This section concerns facilities management for the event you are planning and is not intended as a comprehensive guide to designing or managing facilities. Good planning of facilities is essential to running a successful event. Following the steps listed here will decrease the likelihood of your forgetting an important aspect of facility management for your event.

A. Determine your facility needs.

Your response: *We'll need to use both girls and boys visiting and home team locker rooms. In addition to regular bleacher seating, we'll need to set up additional seating at south end of gym. All gym area restrooms will need to be available. We'll also need maximum ticket taking procedures in place, as well as ushers for the bleachers and the extra south end of gym seating.*

Start date: *now*   Complete date: *January 31*

B. Reserve the facility.

Your response: *Facility reserved.*

C. Determine who will supervise the facility.

Your response: *Check with Matt to see if he can supervise this event. If he can't, check with others to determine availability.*

Start date: *now*   Complete date: *January 31*

E. Prepare the facility prior to the event.

Your response: *Inform custodial crew of any alterations to regular home game set-up. Determine any other special instructions that may not be on the regular home game set-up list. Give administrative staff responsibility for making directional signs.*

Start date: *February 1*   Complete date: *February 7*

F. Arrange for maintenance of the facility.

Your response: *Have maintenance conduct pre-practice facility inspection, as well as pre-event (after practices) inspection. Use modification of Form 12 for these inspections. Because this is a two game event, in addition to regular duties determine other duties and time frame for them. Pass these additional duties on to maintenance and custodial staff.*

Start date: *February 20*   Complete date: *March 3*

H. Arrange for adequate parking if needed.

Your response: *Our parking lots should accommodate all spectators, although we need to obtain permission to use Bel-Air's lot across the street if overflow is needed.*

Start date: *February 15*   Complete date: *February 20*

10. AWARDS AND RECOGNITION PLANS

Everyone likes to be recognized for their accomplishments, yet it is important that awards and recognition are appropriate in sports programs. As you plan your event, decide what types (if any) of awards and recognition you want to offer to the players, teams, coaches, and other helpers. What types of awards are appropriate for the level of competition? As you plan for awards and recognition, think carefully about the contribution of these awards and recognition to your program objectives. If the event is large, consider developing an awards committee to be responsible for the tasks in this category.

A. Determine for what achievements awards will be given and how they will be given.

Your response: *Conference office will be providing all awards.*

D. Plan for the storage of the awards before the event.

Your response: *Awards will be stored in the athletic offices, room 23, before the event and overnight until the first game on Saturday. Paula will transfer awards pre- and post-event.*

E. Plan for the display of the awards during the event.

Your response: *We will set up a table in the south foyer outside the gym to display awards during games. "Roamers" used for the event will take turns staying with awards while they are on display.*

Start date: *March 3*   Complete date: *March 7*

F. Plan for the presentation of awards.

Your response: *Conference commissioner will be here to handle award presentations. After the championship game, award presentations for team and individual accomplishments will take place. The PA system microphone will be ready to go out on floor with commissioner (maintenance staff will adjust after last game).*

G. Plan for recognizing those who have contributed to the event in various ways and implement those plans.

Your response: *Prepare an announcement including a list of individuals to thank. Determine whether commissioner will read this announcement at beginning of award presentations (preferred), or whether I will read introduction and thanks at beginning of award presentations, and then introduce commissioner for team and individual award presentations.*

Start date: *February 27*   Complete date: *March 3*

11. FOOD SERVICE PLANS

Decide what food and drink service you want and need to provide. Of course you will need water for the participants and others, but what beyond that? The sale of food and drinks is one way to raise additional revenue, but doing this requires well-organized service, perhaps a contract with a professional concessionaire. If you get into selling foods, be aware of and in compliance with local health department regulations. Find out about any facility policy regarding having food and drink in gyms or other facilities (indoor and outdoor). Consider if a hospitality tent is needed. If you plan to have extensive food and drink service, you will want to delegate someone to oversee this function.

A. Arrange for drinks for participants.

Your response: _Large jugs of water will be on each team's bench. The trainers will be responsible for monitoring the water level in the jugs and refilling them when necessary._

C. Arrange for refreshments for other personnel.

Your response: _Individuals working the event will each receive four tickets per night for beverages and snacks at the snack bar. Tickets will be distributed at the worker check-in site at the tournament desk. Administrative assistant will make up these refreshment tickets._

Start date: _February 15_   Complete date: _February 22_

D. Arrange for refreshments for spectators.

Your response: _We will offer regular home basketball game concessions, but will need to increase food and beverage stock on hand. Determine stock needed and obtain student and/or booster workers for the concessions._

Start date: _January 22_   Complete date: _January 28_

14. PROMOTION PLANS

Effective promotion has several components. First, you want to let your target audience know about your event. Then, you want to encourage them to either participate or attend. Determining who, what, and how are all important aspects of effectively promoting your event. The following tasks will help you develop your promotion plans.

A. Determine what you want to promote and to whom.

Your response: *We want to promote this event to spectators in our community as well as the communities of the other participating teams.*

C. Prepare the promotional materials.

Your response: *Prepare a radio public service announcement (PSA) and distribute it to stations in communities of participating teams. Have students in art and design class work on posters to promote home team, and then distribute posters in downtown and mall areas of our community. Contact local newspaper, send press release.*

Start date: *February 27*   Complete date: *March 8*

D. Release the promotional materials.

Your response: *Run radio PSAs—March 6 through March 11; distribute posters between March 7 and March 8; send press release on March 6.*

15. PUBLIC RELATIONS PLANS

Public relations is managing the image of your athletic program and the event you are conducting. It is especially important that you address public relations for events in which you want the teams, players, parents, coaches, and other volunteers to participate again. The key to good public relations in high school sports programs is serving participant needs and interests well. For a large event, consider developing a media and public relations committee to oversee and manage all aspects of this category.

B. Plan your PR with coaches, officials, and other volunteer help.

Your response: _Let all coaches, officials, and volunteer help know that any developments will be posted at the tournament desk, located in northeast hall outside the gym. Any immediate breaks of information will be relayed to all concerned parties._

C. Plan your PR with the media.

Your response: _A press table will be provided courtside. It will accommodate two press people from each competing community. All stats will be available one hour after completion of game time at the tournament desk (in northeast hall outside the gym)._

16. COMMUNICATION PLANS

So often we see technically well-organized events break down because of communication problems. Don't assume anything with communication—others can't read your mind. In developing your event plans, don't forget the importance of good communication among yourself, your staff, your participants, and others.

A. Develop a communication system between you and your directors and your directors and their staff.

Your response: _All communication will center on the tournament desk. All workers will be instructed to check in at the desk if any questions/ problems arise during the event._

B. Plan how to communicate with participants and coaches.

Your response: _Coaches will also be required to check in at the tournament desk. Any communications will occur through the tournament desk._

C. Plan a system for communication with spectators.

Your response: _Publish event program with rosters of each team and a brief synopsis of each team's season. Plan introductions of players, coaches, and officials prior to each game._

Start date: _March 5_   Complete date: _March 9_

D. Plan a system for communicating with the media.

Your response: _Assign media relations tasks to communications manager, Kim Berg. Have her determine plan for media communication during event. Get press releases prepared and sent out by March 4._

Start date: _immediately_   Complete date: _March 4_

E. Plan for communicating results to the high school activities/athletic organization or the governing body of the sport.

Your response: *Conference representatives will be here, so they will take care of notifying the conference office. Have media relations communicate results to state activities association and newspapers of participating teams.*

17. EVENT EVALUATION PLAN

Once the event is over, it's still not quite over. A brief evaluation of the event will let you know what worked well and not so well so that you can improve on your next event. If you discover any items that we didn't think to include in this guide, add them to it and let us know so we can improve this tool for all athletic administrators and club team directors.

A. Determine the system for evaluation.

Your response: _Obtain feedback from workers via survey. Also, solicit feedback via survey from various spectators as they wait in the foyer._

B. Prepare the evaluation questionnaire.

Your response: _Prepare worker and spectator evaluation surveys. Use Form 16 as an example._

Start date: _February 1_   Complete date: _February 7_

C. Have the evaluation forms completed by those selected to evaluate the event.

Your response: _Tell workers about evaluations when they check in. Give them the evaluation form when they check out. For spectator evaluations, have a table with sign in the foyer where people can walk up and complete form, as well as having someone pass out surveys after games are over._

D. Review and summarize the evaluation comments.

Your response: _Go through evaluations the following week. Record all pertinent information and file for other events. Also, pass along feedback to those who would benefit from it._

Start date: _March 13_   Complete date: _March 23_

18. STAFFING PLANS

A common mistake of less experienced athletic administrators and directors is failing to staff adequately and being reluctant to ask others for help, leaving an inordinate work load for themselves. The consequence often is that these directors are so busy performing various functions that they neglect their major responsibility—the coordinating and supervising of the other staff. If you are in charge of a large event, the importance of surrounding yourself with competent people cannot be underestimated because delegating responsibility is paramount to running this type of event. Recognize that staffing is not only recruiting the right people but also training, communicating with, motivating, supervising, evaluating, paying, and recognizing those who work with you to conduct the event.

A. Determine the staff required to conduct the event.

Your response: _Form 3 is completed. Refer to it regarding staff needs. Within some categories (Financial, Awards, Promotion, Public Relations, and Communication), manager will be responsible for entire category, determining if others are needed to assist with the category tasks. Need to meet with each of the category managers by February 15._

Start date: _now_   Complete date: _February 10_

B. Recruit the volunteers needed.

Your response: _Need to recruit a volunteer coordinator. Have him or her begin recruiting volunteers to work. The volunteers needed are food preparers, food sellers, and food cleanup workers._

Start date: _immediately_   Complete date: _February 15_

C. Hire the employees needed.

Your response: _I will assume the paid-help coordinator responsibilities. Paid help includes scorekeepers, announcer, maintenance, technical assistant, ticket takers, ushers, parking assistants, locker room security, and "roamers." See budget for fees to pay._

Start date: _immediately_   Complete date: _February 15_

D. Make assignments to all staff.

Your response: *Make sure all category managers know their responsibilities. Meet with all category managers for comprehensive event meeting on February 23 at 7:00 p.m.*

Start date: *immediately*   Complete date: *February 20*

E. Provide orientation and training.

Your response: *Comprehensive event meeting will cover any questions and training needed. Because most of these people are experienced at what they're doing, I'm not anticipating a large amount of new training.*

F. Plan the communication system with staff.

Your response: *Prior to the event, all communication that needs to be directed to all managers will go through me. Tell all who might have something everyone needs to know about to pass on to me. During the event, our tournament desk will serve as the communication center for the event.*

H. Plan for the payment and/or recognition of your staff.

Your response: *Financial manager will take care of prompt payment of paid staff. I will write a letter of appreciation to all others who have assisted with this event.*

Start date: *March 13*   Complete date: *March 20*

 **Form 1**

EVENT PLANNING CHECKLIST

Use this form as you read through the Event Management guide. Consider each category and determine whether or not it applies to your event. Once you've determined this, put a check in the appropriate column. If you aren't sure, check the question mark column and come back to that category once you've gathered more information about your event. If you need more detail regarding a particular category or the tasks within, refer to the page reference where the category can be found. Use the extra spaces at the end of the form to add categories that we have not included (you may not realize what these categories are yet, so don't worry if you have to add them later).

Category	Yes	No	?
1. Planning the event objectives (pages 1–3)	√		
2. Financial planning (pages 4–7)	√		
3. Rules and officials plans (pages 8–10)	√		
4. Coach development plans (pages 11–13)		√	
5. Risk and emergency plans (pages 14–17)	√		
6. Registration plans (pages 18–19)			√
7. Scheduling plans (pages 20–22)	√		
8. Facilities planning (pages 23–26)	√		
9. Equipment, uniforms, and supplies planning (pages 27–29)		√	
10. Awards and recognition plans (pages 30–32)	√		
11. Food service plans (pages 33–34)	√		
12. Transportation plans (pages 35–36)		√	
13. Housing plans (pages 37–38)		√	
14. Promotion plans (pages 39–42)	√		
15. Public relations plans (pages 43–44)	√		
16. Communication plans (pages 45–46)	√		
17. Event evaluation plan (pages 47–48)	√		
18. Staffing plans (pages 49–52)	√		
Additional categories			
19.			
20.			
21.			

 Form 2

FINANCIAL PLANNING FORM
Model for Interscholastic/Club Sport Budget

Use this form to develop a financial plan for your event. You'll look at sources of income and estimated expenditures and compare these figures for a total budget. Directions are included at the beginning of each section of the form. Notice that all sections have an **Actual** column and an **Over/under budget** column. After the event, complete the form by filling in these two columns, and then determining where you were actually over and under budget. Save this worksheet to help you in planning budgets for similar events in the future.

Part I   Sources of Income

In this section you'll determine your sources of income, distinguishing between committed funds (those you know are available to you) and potential funds (good prospects for funds not yet locked up). For each category of funds, calculate a total by adding the committed funds and potential funds for each category.

	Committed ($)	Potential ($)	Total ($)	Actual ($)	Over/under budget ($)
School district funds			0		
Federal and state grants			0		
Registration and entry fees			0		
Participation fees			0		
Admission fees		2050.00*	2050.00		
User fees for facilities and equipment			0		
Concession sales		500.00	500.00		
Other sales			0		
Private gifts and donations			0		
Special event fundraising			0		
Commercial sponsorships			0		
Other _host stipend_	500.00		500.00		
Other _____			0		
Total income	$ 500.00	$2550.00	$3050.00		
	A	B	C		

*100 adults @ $5.00/night × 2 nights = $1000.00
150 students @ $3.50/night × 2 nights = $1050.00
$2050.00

Part II   Sources of Expenditures

In this section, estimate your expenses for conducting this event.

	Budget ($)	Actual ($)	Over/under budget ($)
Personnel expenses	*1970.00**	_____	_____

Subcategories may include full- and part-time employees, officials, coaches, and supervisors. You also will record your benefits expenses here.

Education and training expenses	-0-	_____	_____

These expenses are not included in many club or interscholastic sport budgets, but they should be, just as they are in most companies now. Record here expenses for the education of coaches, parents, and your permanent staff.

Facility expenses	-0-	_____	_____

Subcategories may include facility operating expenses, maintenance, rental payments, and utilities. This category of expense does not include capital expenses for building new facilities or remodeling.

Equipment and uniform expenses	-0-	_____	_____

Each of these could be separate accounts, with purchasing and repair as subaccounts for equipment, and purchase and cleaning as subaccounts for uniforms. If you operate a multisport program, you could divide these accounts further by each sport.

Supplies expenses	*100.00*	_____	_____

These may include office supplies, cleaning supplies, toiletries, and training room/first aid supplies.

Food service expenses	*350.00*	_____	_____

If you provide food or drink without charge, you will need to track these expenses. If you sell food and drink, record the purchase cost of the items sold here.

Housing and transportation expenses	-0-	_____	_____

When your event includes traveling to another city, or providing housing and/or transportation for teams coming to your event, record these expenses here.

Promotion and public relations expenses	*100.00*	_____	_____

These are expenses associated with informing potential participants and volunteers about the events in your program.

*scorekeepers: 3 @ $50/night × 2 nights = $300
announcer: $50/night × 2 nights = $100
maintenance overtime = $250
technical assistant: $30/night × 2 nights = $60
ticket takers: 8 @ $20/night × 2 nights = $320

ushers: 10 @ $15/night × 2 nights = $300
parking assistants: 6 @ $30/night × 2 nights = $360
locker room security: 4 @ $20/night × 2 nights = $160
"roamers": 3 @ $20/night × 2 nights = $120
$1970

Legal and accounting expenses   -0-   _____   _____

This expense category is for any legal work you have done, such as facility leases, sponsorship agreements, review of waiver forms, and any formal litigation action. It is also where you record any expense associated with keeping these records.

Insurance expenses   -0-   _____   _____

These expenses include a wide range of possible insurances you may wish to purchase depending on your situation.

Publications expenses   50.00   _____   _____

Record under this category your costs to prepare schedules, rules, policy manuals, programs, and other materials to communicate with your constituents.

Awards and recognition expenses   -0-   _____   _____

Enter here the purchase cost of trophies, medals, ribbons, certificates, banquet meals, and other forms of recognizing participants and volunteers in the program.

Communication expenses   50.00   _____   _____

Telephone and postage are the two major expenses here.

Other expenses   -0-   _____   _____

Accommodates whatever doesn't fit into the preceding accounts.

Total expenditures $2620.00   _____   _____

D

Part III   Summary

In this section, you'll calculate the difference between the anticipated income and expenses. First you'll need to transfer some figures. The lines are labeled to assist you in doing this.

	Committed ($)	Potential ($)	Budget ($)	Actual ($)	Over/under budget ($)
Total income	$500.00	$2550.00	$3050.00	_____	_____
	A	B	C		
Total expenditures			$2620.00	_____	_____
			D		
Net income/(loss)			$430.00	_____	_____

Compare the committed funds (A) to expenses (D) first. If these funds cover the expenses, then you have no financial worries. If the committed funds do not cover expenses, then determine if the committed and potential funds combined (C) cover your expenses (D). If they do not, you need to develop plans for reducing your expenses or increasing income. If the combination does cover your expenses, calculate the amount that comes from potential funds (B) and give careful thought to the probability of obtaining these funds. Continue revising your budget as you obtain more accurate information about available funds and actual expenses.

 **Form 3**

STAFF PLANNING FORM

Keep this Staff Planning Form handy as you complete your event management plan. Review the list of positions—they correspond to the categories of the Event Management guide. Mark out those not needed for your event. On this form only enter the manager's name for each planning category and not the names of the support staff. We assume you will have only one manager for each category. Often the same person will be the manager for several categories. Indicate the number of support staff needed prior to the event and the number of work hours needed from each, as well as the number needed during the event and the number of work hours needed from each. Insert in the "Other" space position titles for additional personnel needed.

Position	Pre-event #	Pre-event Hours	Event #	Event Hours
Event director _Dave Stone_				
Event planning assistant			1	12
Clerical assistant	1	ongoing		
Computer assistant				
Other _____				
Other _____				
Financial manager _Paula Wilson_				
Fundraisers				
Other _____				
Other _____				
Rules and officials manager _Dave Stone_				
Officials (umpires, referees)*_covered by conference office_				
Scorekeepers			3	12
Timers				
Judges				
Announcers			1	12
Other _law enforcement_			4	12
Other _____				
Coaching manager _____				
Coaches				
Assistant coaches				
Team statisticians				
Other _____				
Other _____				

Position	Pre-event		Event	
	#	Hours	#	Hours
Risk manager _Dave Stone_				
Physicians			1	12
Trainers			2	28
Other _____				
Other _____				
Registration manager _____				
Registration clerks				
Check-in manager				
Other _____				
Other _____				
Scheduling manager _Dave Stone_				
Other _____				
Other _____				
Facility manager _Matt Hossell_				
Facility supervisor			1	12
Facility maintenance workers	4	6	4	12
Technical assistants			1	12
Ticket takers			8	10
Ushers			10	12
Parking assistants			6	6
Other _locker room security_			4	12
Other _"roamers"_			3	12
Event equipment manager _Dave Stone_				
Site equipment manager				
Other _____				
Other _____				
Awards manager _Paula Wilson_				
Awards presenters				
Other _____				
Other _____				
Food manager _Kasey Estaff_				
Food preparers	2	3	2	12
Food sellers			3	12
Food cleanup workers			3	2
Other _____				
Other _____				

Position	Pre-event		Event	
	#	Hours	#	Hours
Transportation manager _____				
Drivers	___	___	___	___
Other _____	___	___	___	___
Other _____	___	___	___	___
Housing manager _____				
Other _____	___	___	___	___
Other _____	___	___	___	___
Promotion manager _Paula Wilson_				
Merchandise seller	___	___	___	___
Other _____	___	___	___	___
Other _____	___	___	___	___
Public relations manager _Steve Dawe_				
Photographer	___	___	___	___
Publications assistant (programs, brochures)	___	___	___	___
Other _____	___	___	___	___
Other _____	___	___	___	___
Communications manager _Kim Berg_				
Other _____	___	___	___	___
Other _____	___	___	___	___
Event evaluation manager _Dave Stone_				
Other _____	___	___	___	___
Other _____	___	___	___	___
Staffing manager _Dave Stone_				
Volunteer coordinator	1	20	1	12
Paid help coordinator	1	20	1	12
Gate help coordinator	1	10	1	12
Scorekeeper manager			1	12
Other _____	___	___	___	___
Other _____	___	___	___	___

 **Form 7**

DESIGNING YOUR RISK MANAGEMENT PLAN

Follow the steps of this exercise to create a risk management plan for your event. Take your time and be thorough about completing it. It could pay off by preventing an injury and/or a lawsuit.

Step 1. The first thing you want to do is determine specific potential risks. The accompanying two checklists of general risks will serve as a starting point to help you identify possible risks. Use the first checklist, Checklist of Event Risks, if you are running an event such as a tournament, interclub, or interscholastic competition. If you are planning league play across the season, use the second checklist, the Checklist of General Risks in Sport.

Checklist of Event Risks

Identify the risks in conducting this event by answering Yes or No to the following questions:

Have you ensured . . .

	Yes	No
proper supervision in all areas utilized by the event?	☑	☐
a plan for occurrence of adverse weather conditions?	☑	☐
safety checks for playing areas?	☑*	☐
checks for defective or unsafe equipment?	☑	☐
facility maintenance before and during event?	☑	☐
plans for emergencies affecting all in attendance (spectators, workers, participants)?	☑	☐
plans for attending to participants' first aid/medical emergencies?	☑	☐
injury report plans?	☑	☐
the attendance of appropriate medical personnel/supplies?	☑	☐
fair and equitable opportunities for all participants?	☑	☐
qualified officials and other event personnel?	☑	☐
proper spectator facilities?	☑	☐
protected areas for spectators?	☑	☐
a system for warning spectators of any possible risks? *(not applicable)*	☐	☐
proof of insurance for any drivers providing transportation? *(not applicable)*	☐	☐

Possible risk—water fountain jutting out of wall at north end of court.

Checklist of General Risks in Sport

Identify the general risks in your sport program by answering Yes or No to the following questions:

Do coaches . . .

	Yes	No
provide a safe environment for practice and contests?	☐	☐
teach skills in developmentally appropriate progressions?	☐	☐
provide appropriate supervision for activities?	☐	☐
warn players of inherent risks in the activity?	☐	☐
enforce the rules and regulations of the sport and your organization?	☐	☐
match and equate players fairly for practice and contests?	☐	☐
provide proper first aid when injuries occur?	☐	☐
keep records of injuries and other emergencies?	☐	☐
ensure the civil rights of all participants?	☐	☐
understand the difference between ordinary negligence and gross negligence?	☐	☐
know the signs and symptoms of possible child abuse?	☐	☐
know that by law they must report to the appropriate authorities any reason they have to believe any vulnerable individual is being abused or neglected?	☐	☐
know whether the immunity laws in your state protect them against ordinary negligence?	☐	☐
know if they are covered under your organization's insurance program?	☐	☐
have a plan for obtaining medical assistance?	☐	☐
submit reports on all injuries and accidents?	☐	☐
transport participants using their personal vehicles?	☐	☐

Do you . . .

	Yes	No
follow a formal procedure for selecting qualified staff, officials, and coaches to conduct the program?	☐	☐
ensure that your staff, officials, and coaches are appropriately educated to perform their duties?	☐	☐
monitor all aspects of the program appropriately, especially the competitive events and the facilities in which they occur?	☐	☐
keep up-to-date job descriptions that define the coaches' duties?	☐	☐
supervise, evaluate, and provide feedback to your coaches about how to perform their duties?	☐	☐
honor equal employment opportunity guidelines when hiring or terminating a coach?	☐	☐
follow ADA mandates that policies, procedures, and practices that discriminate against the disabled population be eliminated?	☐	☐

Do you . . .

	Yes	No
keep your risk management plan up-to-date?	☐	☐
ensure that you and your staff are knowledgeable about certain standards regarding sports facilities and equipment purchasing and maintenance?	☐	☐
keep up-to-date with health, physical education, and medical organizations that offer recommendations on safe practices in sport, recommended ages for participation, conditions that disqualify participants from participation, preparticipation physical examinations, strength and conditioning guidelines, and drug use?	☐	☐
receive periodicals that provide coverage of risk management issues?	☐	☐
educate your staff and coaches?	☐	☐
supervise all aspects of your program or assign others to provide general and specific supervision?	☐	☐
assign others to supervise a playing facility or special event only after making sure they are competent to plan for the activity?	☐	☐
ensure that your staff members follow guidelines and a checklist for supervising sports facilities?	☐	☐
keep up-to-date supervision guidelines for all your programs?	☐	☐
ensure that all staff members follow guidelines and use a checklist for supervising the use of sports equipment?	☐	☐
maintain a careful system of record keeping that could serve as legal documentation in case of a lawsuit?	☐	☐
ensure that the parents of the participants in your program assume risk by signing waivers/releases and consent forms?	☐	☐
ensure that your organization purchases all the types of insurance it needs for staff and coaches?	☐	☐
keep an up-to-date Emergency Medical Response Plan that you developed in consultation with a local physician, preferably a sports medicine specialist?	☐	☐
require all participants to provide you with a medical history?	☐	☐
require all participants to have a preparticipation physical examination to identify potential medical problems?	☐	☐
ensure that all participants fill out an emergency information card?	☐	☐
train your coaches and supervisors about what to do and what not to do when players are injured?	☐	☐
ensure that all athletes in your programs are transported by licensed commercial carriers?	☐	☐
ensure that athletes who are not transported this way are transported instead by vehicles of your agency?	☐	☐
ensure that all drivers of your agency's vehicles are qualified?	☐	☐
ensure that the vehicles are in good repair and properly insured?	☐	☐
keep up-to-date policies to ensure that all personnel and athletes in your program are afforded due process?	☐	☐

Step 2.   List each risk in your program by describing it under the "Source of risk" heading on the following form. You are considering two major types of risk: risk to the well-being of your participants and spectators; and risk to you, your staff, and volunteers with regard to legal liability and thus financial loss.

Your Risk Management Plan

Source of risk:

Unsupervised attendees (kids) playing underneath bleachers and in hallways.

Probability of occurrence: (Low)   Moderate   High

Severity if it occurs: Low   (Moderate)   High

Method to reduce risk:

Assign personnel ("roamers") to check underneath bleachers occasionally; check hallways in school to make sure no one is out of place.

Source of risk:

Athlete who is running out of bounds on north end of gym hitting protruding water fountain near corner of court.

Probability of occurrence: Low   (Moderate)   High

Severity if it occurs: Low   (Moderate)   High

Method to reduce risk:

Discuss possibility of placing one or two mats over fountain. Maintenance could do this on Friday a.m. and take them down on Saturday or Sunday, postevent.

Step 3.   For each risk you listed on the "Source of risk" form, determine the probability of the risk occurring and circle "High," "Moderate," or "Low" on the form. You may want to obtain the opinion of others about the probability of the risk occurring if you have minimal experience.

Step 4.   Next, estimate the potential severity of this risk should it occur and indicate the degree of severity by circling "High," "Moderate," or "Low."

Step 5.   Now for the critical step: Can you best deal with this risk in some way by (a) avoiding the risk, (b) reducing the risk, or (c) transferring the risk? Write down in the space provided the actions you believe best in your situation.

Implement your recommendations to alleviate the risk, communicate the plan to alert all those who need to know, and continually monitor the plan to add items missed in your initial evaluation.

Form 12

FACILITY INSPECTION CHECKLIST FOR BASKETBALL CONFERENCE TOURNAMENT

This form is provided as a sample facility inspection checklist and is designed to help you develop a checklist specific for your facilities. This is an incomplete checklist.

Name of inspector _____

Date of inspection _____

Name and location of facility _____

_____

Note: This is an incomplete checklist; it is provided as an example and is designed to help you develop a checklist specific for your facilities.

Facility Condition

Circle Y (yes) if the facility is in good condition and N (no) if it needs something done to make it acceptable. Fill in what needs to be done on the line to the right.

Gymnasium

Y   N   Floor (no water spots, buckling, loose sections) _____

Y   N   Walls (vandalism free) _____

Y   N   Lights (all functioning) _____

Y   N   Windows (secure) _____

Y   N   Roof (no adverse impact of weather) _____

Y   N   Stairs (well lighted) _____

Y   N   Bleachers (support structure sound) _____

Y   N   Exits (lights working) _____

Y   N   Basketball rims (level, securely attached) _____

Y   N   Basketball backboards (no cracks, clean) _____

Y   N   Mats (clean, properly stored, no defects) _____

Y   N   Uprights/projections _____

Y   N   Wall plugs (covered) _____

Y   N   Light switches (all functioning) _____

Y   N   Heating/cooling system (temperature control) _____

Y   N   Ducts, radiators, pipes _____

Y   N   Thermostats _____

Y   N   Fire alarms (regularly checked) _____

Y   N   Directions posted for evacuating the gym in case of fire ____

Y   N   Fire extinguishers (regularly checked) _____

Other (list) _____

_____

Locker Room(s)

Y   N   Floor _____

Y   N   Walls _____

Y   N   Lights _____

Y   N   Windows _____

Y   N   Roof _____

Y   N   Showers _____

Y   N   Drains _____

Y   N   Benches _____

Y   N   Lockers _____

Y   N   Exits _____

Y   N   Water fountains _____

Y   N   Toilets _____

Y   N   Trainer's room _____

Other (list) _____

_____

Concession area

Y   N   Electrical _____

Y   N   Heating/cooling systems _____

Other (list) _____

_____

Emergency telephone lights and public address system

Y   N   Accessible _____

Y   N   Directions for use visibly posted _____

Y   N   Powered by emergency generators as well as regular power system _____

Y   N   Emergency numbers on telephone cradle or receiver _____

Emergency procedures

Y   N   Sign posted in highly visible area _____

Recommendations/observations: _____

_____

_____

◤▪ Form 12

FACILITY INSPECTION CHECKLIST FOR BASKETBALL CONFERENCE TOURNAMENT

This form is provided as a sample facility inspection checklist and is designed to help you develop a checklist specific for your facilities. This is an incomplete checklist.

Name of inspector _____

Date of inspection _____

Name and location of facility _____

_____

Note: This is an incomplete checklist; it is provided as an example and is designed to help you develop a checklist specific for your facilities.

Facility Condition

Circle Y (yes) if the facility is in good condition and N (no) if it needs something done to make it acceptable. Fill in what needs to be done on the line to the right.

Gymnasium

Y   N   Floor (no water spots, buckling, loose sections) _____

Y   N   Walls (vandalism free) _____

Y   N   Lights (all functioning) _____

Y   N   Windows (secure) _____

Y   N   Roof (no adverse impact of weather) _____

Y   N   Stairs (well lighted) _____

Y   N   Bleachers (support structure sound) _____

Y   N   Exits (lights working) _____

Y   N   Basketball rims (level, securely attached) _____

Y   N   Basketball backboards (no cracks, clean)_____

Y   N   Mats (clean, properly stored, no defects) _____

Y   N   Uprights/projections _____

Y   N   Wall plugs (covered)_____

Y   N   Light switches (all functioning) _____

Y   N   Heating/cooling system (temperature control) _____

Y   N   Ducts, radiators, pipes _____

Y   N   Thermostats _____

Y   N   Fire alarms (regularly checked) _____

Y   N   Directions posted for evacuating the gym in case of fire _____

Y   N   Fire extinguishers (regularly checked) _____

Other (list) _____

_____

Locker Room(s)

Y   N   Floor _____

Y   N   Walls _____

Y   N   Lights _____

Y   N   Windows _____

Y   N   Roof _____

Y   N   Showers _____

Y   N   Drains _____

Y   N   Benches _____

Y   N   Lockers _____

Y   N   Exits _____

Y   N   Water fountains _____

Y   N   Toilets _____

Y   N   Trainer's room _____

Other (list) _____

_____

Concession area

Y   N   Electrical _____

Y   N   Heating/cooling systems _____

Other (list) _____

_____

Emergency telephone lights and public address system

Y   N   Accessible _____

Y   N   Directions for use visibly posted _____

Y   N   Powered by emergency generators as well as regular power system _____

Y   N   Emergency numbers on telephone cradle or receiver_____

Emergency procedures

Y   N   Sign posted in highly visible area_____

Recommendations/observations: _____

_____

_____

Item	Item number	Unit price*
NFICEP Coaching Principles Videotape Set (5)	MNFI0100	325.00
Coaching Philosophy Videotape	MNFI0101	70.00
Sport Psychology Videotape	MNFI0102	70.00
Sport Pedagogy Videotape	MNFI0103	70.00
Sport Physiology Videotape	MNFI0104	70.00
Sport Management Videotape	MNFI0105	70.00

Leader Level Sport First Aid Course Materials

Item	Item number	Unit price*
Leader Level Sport First Aid Course (*Sport First Aid*, *Clinic Study Guide*, Course Processing, Diploma)	ACEP0081	30.00
Sport First Aid	PFLE0410	18.00
Sport First Aid Instructor Guide	ACEP0004	70.00
Sport First Aid Clinic Study Guide (package of 10)	ACEP0036	22.50
Sport First Aid Leadership Training Seminar	ACEP0068	199.00
Leader Level Sport First Aid Videotape	MACE0106	125.00

NFICEP Sport First Aid Course Materials

Item	Item number	Unit price*
NFICEP Sport First Aid Course (*Sport First Aid*, *Clinic Study Guide*, Course Processing, Diploma)	ACEP0082	30.00
Sport First Aid (NFICEP Edition)	ACEP0065	18.00
Sport First Aid Instructor Guide	ACEP0006	70.00
Sport First Aid Leadership Training Seminar	ACEP0070	199.00
Leader Level Sport First Aid Videotape	MNFI0106	125.00

Leader Level/NFICEP Drugs and Sport Course Materials

Item	Item number	Unit price*
Coaches Guide to Drugs and Sport	PRIN0715	17.95

Leader Level Sport Techniques and Tactics Resources

Item	Item number	Unit price*
Coaching Basketball Successfully	PWOO0446	18.95
Coaching Girls' Basketball Successfully	PHUT0343	20.00
Coaching Football Successfully	PREA0518	18.95
Coaching Swimming Successfully	PHAN0492	18.95
Coaching Tennis Successfully	PUST0461	18.95
Coaching Volleyball Successfully	PNEV0362	18.00

Leader Level SportDirector Resources

Item	Item number	Unit price*
Event Management for SportDirectors	ACEP0320	20.00
Program Evaluation for SportDirectors	PKES0505	20.00
Promotion for SportDirectors	PJOH0722	20.00

*ALL PRICES ARE SUBJECT TO CHANGE. Call ASEP at (800) 747-5698 for current price information.

American Sport Education Program

Leader Level

ASEP's Leader Level provides quality resources and courses for coaches and administrators in interscholastic and club sport. In fact, the National Federation of State High School Associations has selected the Leader Level SportCoach Courses as its own coaches education program, called NFICEP–National Federation Interscholastic Coaches Education Program. The Leader Level offers the following:

▲ Leadership Training Seminars

Our Leadership Training Seminars (LTSs) not only show sport administrators how to conduct our courses, they also revitalize them with fresh ideas about how to help coaches be more effective in their coaching roles. Leader Level instructor seminars include the

- Coaching Principles Seminar,
- Sport First Aid Seminar, and
- Drugs and Sport Seminar (in development).

▲ Coaches Courses

Once administrators have attended our LTSs, they are prepared to teach our **Coaching Principles Course** and **Sport First Aid Course,** and soon, the **Drugs and Sport Course** to coaches. The courses provide excellent educational opportunities for both new and experienced coaches. At each course, coaches attend a clinic, study the course text and study guide, then take an open-book test.

▲ The Coaching Successfully Series

The books in this series explain how to teach fundamental sports skills and strategies as well as how to build a sports program by applying principles of philosophy, psychology, and teaching and management methods to coaching.

Series Titles

- Coaching Tennis Successfully
- Coaching Swimming Successfully
- Coaching Football Successfully
- Coaching Basketball Successfully
- Coaching Volleyball Successfully
- Coaching Girls' Basketball Successfully
- Coaching Baseball Successfully

▲ SportDirector Series

See facing page for information.

For more information about ASEP and the Leader Level, call toll-free 1-800-747-5698.

 **Form 16**

SAMPLE EVENT EVALUATION FORM

Please complete the following evaluation and return it to us before leaving this event. Your comments will help us to improve future events. Thanks for your input!

Rate the quality of	Low				High
the overall event	1	2	3	4	5
competition	1	2	3	4	5
event organization	1	2	3	4	5
scheduling	1	2	3	4	5
event staff	1	2	3	4	5
parking	1	2	3	4	5
officiating	1	2	3	4	5
facilities	1	2	3	4	5
food and beverage service	1	2	3	4	5
transportation	1	2	3	4	5
housing	1	2	3	4	5
communication between staff and participants	1	2	3	4	5
communication between staff and spectators	1	2	3	4	5

Please use this space to provide any other feedback regarding this event.

Thanks for your input!

Appendix B
American Sport Education Program (ASEP) Leader Level Resources

Item	Item number	Unit price*
Leader Level Coaching Principles Course Materials		
Leader Level Coaching Principles Course (*Successful Coaching, Clinic Study Guide*, Course Processing, Diploma)	ACEP0080	30.00
Successful Coaching	PMAR0376	18.00
Coaching Principles Instructor Guide (Rev. 3rd Ed.)	ACEP0007	70.00
Coaching Principles Clinic Study Guide (package of 10)	ACEP0033	22.50
Coaching Principles Leadership Training Seminar	ACEP0056	299.00
Leader Level Coaching Principles Videotape Set (5)	MACE0100	325.00
Coaching Philosophy Videotape	MACE0101	70.00
Sport Psychology Videotape	MACE0102	70.00
Sport Pedagogy Videotape	MACE0103	70.00
Sport Physiology Videotape	MACE0104	70.00
Sport Management Videotape	MACE0105	70.00
NFICEP Coaching Principles Course Materials		
NFICEP Coaching Principles Course (*Successful Coaching, Clinic Study Guide*, Course Processing, Diploma)	ACEP0083	30.00
Successful Coaching (NFICEP Edition)	ACEP0064	18.00
Coaching Principles Instructor Guide	ACEP0005	70.00
Coaching Principles Leadership Training Seminar	ACEP0058	299.00

Other Resources in the SportDirector Series

Program Evaluation for SportDirectors
James Kestner

1996 • Paper • Approx 120 pp • Item PKES0505
ISBN 0-87322-505-X • $20.00 ($29.95 Canadian)

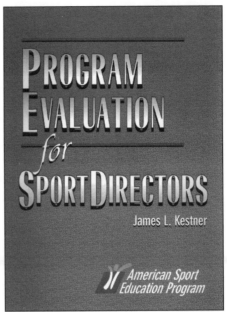

Program Evaluation for SportDirectors is a practical, hands-on resource that you can use to evaluate your personnel, facilities and equipment, and program offerings. It contains an easy-to-follow blueprint for conducting evaluations and 20 field-tested forms that can be used or modified to fit your specific evaluation needs.

First, you'll learn how to prepare for an effective program evaluation. The book explains how to reflect on personal and organizational philosophies, identify who will help in the evaluation process, assess which programs and individuals need to be evaluated, develop an evaluation plan, implement the plan, and review and revise the plan.

The heart of the book shows you how to conduct the actual evaluations. You'll learn to conduct personnel evaluations and discover new methods for evaluating facilities, equipment, and athletic programs. In addition to providing checklists and surveys, the book offers helpful ideas on organizing and keeping records and how to examine the cost effectiveness of programs.

Promotion for SportDirectors
John R. Johnson

1996 • Paper • Approx 144 pp • Item PJOH0722
ISBN 0-87322-722-0 • $20.00 ($29.95 Canadian)

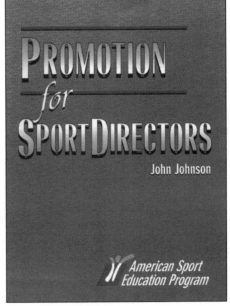

This one-of-a-kind resource will help you properly promote your high school's athletic program and give it the visibility it deserves! The book not only reviews all the promotional tools that are at your disposal, but also explains how to make them an integral part of your program's daily operations.

First, you'll learn how to plan for an effective promotion program. You'll discover how your school's philosophy about promotion meshes with your own, how to assess your promotion needs and limitations, and how to develop a comprehensive promotional plan.

You'll also learn how to implement a positive public relations program, develop and distribute printed promotions such as programs and schedules, take advantage of radio and television promotion, boost attendance using special promotions, and obtain program sponsorships.

2335

131